An Analysis of

John W. Dower's
War Without Mercy:
Race and Power in the Pacific War

Vincent Sánchez
with
Jason Xidias

Routledge
Taylor & Francis Group

LONDON AND NEW YORK

Published by Macat International Ltd
24:13 Coda Centre, 189 Munster Road, London SW6 6AW.

Distributed exclusively by Routledge
4 Park Square, Milton Park, Abingdon, Oxon OX14 4RN
605 Third Avenue, New York, NY 10017

Routledge is an imprint of the Taylor & Francis Group, an informa business

www.macat.com
info@macat.com

Cataloguing in Publication Data
A catalogue record for this book is available from the British Library.
Library of Congress Cataloguing-in-Publication Data is available upon request.
Cover illustration: Etienne Gilfillan

ISBN 978-1-912302-51-2 (hardback)
ISBN 978-1-912128-84-6 (paperback)
ISBN 978-1-912281-39-8 (e-book)

Notice
The information in this book is designed to orientate readers of the work under analysis,
to elucidate and contextualise its key ideas and themes, and to aid in the development
of critical thinking skills. It is not meant to be used, nor should it be used, as a
substitute for original thinking or in place of original writing or research. References and
notes are provided for informational purposes and their presence does not constitute
endorsement of the information or opinions therein. This book is presented solely for
educational purposes. It is sold on the understanding that the publisher is not engaged
to provide any scholarly advice. The publisher has made every effort to ensure that
this book is accurate and up-to-date, but makes no warranties or representations with
regard to the completeness or reliability of the information it contains. The information
and the opinions provided herein are not guaranteed or warranted to produce particular
results and may not be suitable for students of every ability. The publisher shall not be
liable for any loss, damage or disruption arising from any errors or omissions, or from
the use of this book, including, but not limited to, special, incidental, consequential or
other damages caused, or alleged to have been caused, directly or indirectly, by the
information contained within.

CONTENTS

THE MACAT LIBRARY

The Macat Library is a series of unique academic explorations of seminal works in the humanities and social sciences – books and papers that have had a significant and widely recognised impact on their disciplines. It has been created to serve as much more than just a summary of what lies between the covers of a great book. It illuminates and explores the influences on, ideas of, and impact of that book. Our goal is to offer a learning resource that encourages critical thinking and fosters a better, deeper understanding of important ideas.

Each publication is divided into three Sections: Influences, Ideas, and Impact. Each Section has four Modules. These explore every important facet of the work, and the responses to it.

This Section-Module structure makes a Macat Library book easy to use, but it has another important feature. Because each Macat book is written to the same format, it is possible (and encouraged!) to cross-reference multiple Macat books along the same lines of inquiry or research. This allows the reader to open up interesting interdisciplinary pathways.

To further aid your reading, lists of glossary terms and people mentioned are included at the end of this book (these are indicated by an asterisk [*] throughout) – as well as a list of works cited.

Macat has worked with the University of Cambridge to identify the elements of critical thinking and understand the ways in which six different skills combine to enable effective thinking.
Three allow us to fully understand a problem; three more give us the tools to solve it. Together, these six skills make up the **PACIER** model of critical thinking. They are:

ANALYSIS – understanding how an argument is built
EVALUATION – exploring the strengths and weaknesses of an argument
INTERPRETATION – understanding issues of meaning

CREATIVE THINKING – coming up with new ideas and fresh connections
PROBLEM-SOLVING – producing strong solutions
REASONING – creating strong arguments

To find out more, visit **WWW.MACAT.COM.**

CRITICAL THINKING AND *WAR WITHOUT MERCY*

Primary critical thinking skill: PROBLEM-SOLVING
Secondary critical thinking skill: REASONING

John Dower's *War Without Mercy* is an attempt to resolve the problem of why the United States fought World War II so very differently in the Pacific and European theaters. Specifically, the author sets out to explain why there was such vicious hostility between the US and Japan during the conflict. This was not merely a matter of outrage at Pearl Harbor, and understanding the phenomenon required going beyond the usual strategic, diplomatic and operational records that fuel most histories of war. Dower looked instead for alternate possibilities – and found them.

His book argues that the viciousness that marked fighting in the Pacific had deep roots in popular culture which created frightening racial stereotypes of the enemy on both sides of the ocean. Dower's focus on 'low culture' proved to be a useful way of generating alternative possibilities to mainstream thinking about US–Japanese relations. The thinking underpinning the book was innovative, and was challenged by some peers who failed to recognise how profoundly revealing material such as cartoons and cheap magazines could be. But the result was one of the most significant studies of 20th-century history yet written – one that yields a strong, well-reasoned and persuasive solution to the problem posed.

ABOUT THE AUTHOR OF THE ORIGINAL WORK

Born in 1938, **John Dower** is a renowned historian of Japanese-American relations, a Pulitzer Prize winning author, and an emeritus professor at the Massachusetts Institute of Technology (MIT). His pioneering approach focuses on popular culture, and his bold challenges to conventional thought about the Pacific War and racial stereotypes have earned him a place as one of the key thinkers in his field. Dower was also the Executive Producer of the Academy Award nominated 1986 documentary *Hellfire: A Journey from Hiroshima*.

ABOUT THE AUTHORS OF THE ANALYSIS

Vincent Sanchez holds a masters degree in modern history from the University of Chicago.

Dr Jason Xidias holds a PhD in European Politics from King's College London, where he completed a comparative dissertation on immigration and citizenship in Britain and France. He was also a Visiting Fellow in European Politics at the University of California, Berkeley. Currently, he is Lecturer in Political Science at New York University.

ABOUT MACAT

GREAT WORKS FOR CRITICAL THINKING

Macat is focused on making the ideas of the world's great thinkers accessible and comprehensible to everybody, everywhere, in ways that promote the development of enhanced critical thinking skills.

It works with leading academics from the world's top universities to produce new analyses that focus on the ideas and the impact of the most influential works ever written across a wide variety of academic disciplines. Each of the works that sit at the heart of its growing library is an enduring example of great thinking. But by setting them in context – and looking at the influences that shaped their authors, as well as the responses they provoked – Macat encourages readers to look at these classics and game-changers with fresh eyes. Readers learn to think, engage and challenge their ideas, rather than simply accepting them.

'Macat offers an amazing first-of-its-kind tool for interdisciplinary learning and research. Its focus on works that transformed their disciplines and its rigorous approach, drawing on the world's leading experts and educational institutions, opens up a world-class education to anyone.'

Andreas Schleicher
Director for Education and Skills, Organisation for Economic
Co-operation and Development

'Macat is taking on some of the major challenges in university education ... They have drawn together a strong team of active academics who are producing teaching materials that are novel in the breadth of their approach.'

Prof Lord Broers,
former Vice-Chancellor of the University of Cambridge

'The Macat vision is exceptionally exciting. It focuses upon new modes of learning which analyse and explain seminal texts which have profoundly influenced world thinking and so social and economic development. It promotes the kind of critical thinking which is essential for any society and economy. This is the learning of the future.'

Rt Hon Charles Clarke, former UK Secretary of State for Education

'The Macat analyses provide immediate access to the critical conversation surrounding the books that have shaped their respective discipline, which will make them an invaluable resource to all of those, students and teachers, working in the field.'

Professor William Tronzo, University of California at San Diego

WAYS IN TO THE TEXT

KEY POINTS

- John Dower is a renowned historian of Japanese-American relations, the winner of several literary prizes, including the Pulitzer Prize, and an emeritus professor at the Massachusetts Institute of Technology (MIT).

- In his 1986 book *War Without Mercy* Dower argues that, during World War II,* popular culture in both the United States and Japan cast the enemy as a subhuman target that needed to be exterminated.

- In its novel approach of analyzing history through popular music, movies, and even comics, the book was the first major work to link the dehumanizing effects of racism with the extremely brutal undercurrent in Japanese-American relations during World War II.

Who Is John Dower?

John Dower, the author of *War Without Mercy* (1986), was born in Providence, Rhode Island in 1938. He completed a Bachelor of Arts degree in American studies at Amherst College in 1959, a Master of Arts in East Asian studies in 1961, and a PhD in History and Far Eastern Language at Harvard University in 1972. Dower's doctoral thesis—a scholarly but highly readable biography of the controversial Japanese Prime Minster Yoshida Shigeru*—

was published as *Empire and Aftermath* in 1979.

Dower has written a number of important works on Japanese and American history, the most prominent of which are *War Without Mercy* (1986) and *Embracing Defeat* (1999). He was also the executive producer of the Academy Award-nominated documentary *Hellfire: A Journey from Hiroshima*, which portrays the devastating effects that America's dropping of the atomic bomb in 1945 had on the Japanese people.

Dower was a professor of history at the University of Nebraska-Lincoln for eight years, the University of Wisconsin-Madison for six years, and the University of California-San Diego, where he remained until his retirement in 2010. Currently, he is the Ford International Professor of History, Emeritus at MIT. His pioneering approach to cultural history* (roughly, the interpretation of historical events through the lens of past culture) and his compelling writing style have earned him several accolades, including prestigious literary awards such as the National Book Award for Nonfiction, the Pulitzer Prize for General Nonfiction, and the Bancroft Prize.

Dower is also the co-founder of MIT's online project "Visualizing Cultures." Launched in 2002, this collaborative, multi-media initiative uses visual art to engage with modern Japanese and Chinese history.

What Does *War Without Mercy* Say?

War Without Mercy has greatly improved our knowledge and understanding of Japanese-American relations during World War II, and sheds light on the links between popular culture, stereotypes, and violence. The text focuses on the conflict between the United States and Japan, and argues that its racist underpinnings helped make the battles that took place in the Asia-Pacific region known as the Pacific War* (1941–5) a particularly brutal theater of horrors.

American-Japanese relations were relatively cordial until the

1930s. From that point onwards, Japan made aggressive attempts to expand its influence in Asia. Concerned by this, America and its allies attempted to impede this expansion. The period of commercial tension that followed ultimately culminated in Japan's surprise attack on Pearl Harbor* in 1941, America's entry into World War II and the subsequent bombing of Hiroshima* and Nagasaki*—the first use of nuclear weapons in military conflict.

As tensions rose between the United States and Japan, politicians and popular culture created a widespread racial stereotype of the enemy which affected the mindset of ordinary people in both countries. Music, movies, cartoons, and news media popularized and, to a great extent, normalized for their audience the idea of the enemy as subhuman savages. For the Japanese, Americans were portrayed as quintessentially evil, while the Japanese themselves represented all that was pure and honorable. And for Americans, the Japanese were nothing more than irrational animals, while the United States was the epitome of civilization and freedom.

With the full spectrum of popular media (including the influential Japanese comic genre, manga*) depicting the enemy nation as apes, rats, and other vermin, popular culture helped nourish a psychological distancing from the enemy. Supported by this caustic symbolism, Dower persuasively argues that, "the natural response to such a vision was an obsession with extermination on both sides."[1]

Racist imagery of the enemy as subhuman and savage, Dower argues, both legitimized gratuitous violence against the enemy and reinforced both sides' view of the other as lacking basic humanity. Armed with a dangerous dehumanized perception and psychological distancing of their enemy, Japanese and American soldiers slaughtered one another with an intense and merciless hatred. Dower supports this analysis through political cartoons, startling images, and testimonials from military and civilian survivors of the war. Disturbing anecdotes implicate American GIs—soldiers—in sending Japanese skulls, noses, ears, and other gruesome trophies home to their proud wives. Others talked of Japanese soldiers firing on unarmed American prisoners and viciously bayoneting them. News of these unthinkable, and unethical, acts quickly circulated on both the home front and the battlefield. The racial stereotypes that were promoted by both sides throughout the war unofficially sanctioned these extreme violent acts against the enemy, while the atrocities committed by each side only served to confirm popular racial stereotypes. A vicious circle of racism and atrocity developed, each fueling and intensifying the other.

Dower persuasively argues that stereotypes of the Self (us) and the Other* (them) have a long, continuous history through ideas and images that are easily transferrable to a new enemy once hostilities cease.[2] Subject to a constitution authored by the United States, the conquered Japanese quickly became American allies after World War II, seeking to rebuild economically and requiring US military protection following the dissolution of their own armed forces. During the post-war years, Soviet communism* emerged as the United States' most hated Other. This made Japan a strategically important ally for the US in its effort to spread capitalism and liberal democracy,* and to contain Soviet influence and the spread of communism in Asia.

As the US and Soviet Union's ideological and economic rivalry solidified into the decades-long stand-off known as the Cold War,* these two nations each began to generate a similar arsenal of distancing, dehumanizing imagery about each other. Dower's broader argument, therefore, is that racial stereotypes do not disappear, but simply transfer to new enemies. In a world almost continually engaged in conflict with opponents, it is both encouraging and at the same time alarming how quickly enemies turn to allies, and vice versa.

The controversial nature of Dower's analysis, which focuses on the link between racial stereotyping and extreme violence, attracted significant national attention in 1995. During an exhibition at the

National Air and Space Museum in Washington commemorating the 50th anniversary of the dropping of the atomic bomb on Hiroshima and Nagasaki, one artwork echoed Dower's interpretation of the unprecedented bombing as racially motivated. Some participants interpreted Dower's criticism of the atomic bombing as unnecessarily provocative, and, moreover, unpatriotic.

Why Does *War Without Mercy* Matter?

War Without Mercy made a groundbreaking contribution to our understanding of the links between popular culture, stereotypes, and violence during World War II. The author points out that prior to its publication in 1986, racism was "one of the great neglected subjects of World War II."[3] The text has influenced a generation of scholars who have engaged with the topic of racism in Japanese-American relations and the social sciences more broadly. Other studies that have developed out of Dower's work include those that further evaluate the impact of anti-Japanese racism on America's decision to drop the atomic bomb on Hiroshima and Nagasaki in 1945, as well as the large-scale internment of Japanese Americans during the war. His focus on imagery in films, art, cartoons, and other visual media has also had an important influence in film studies.

Dower has written several other significant works on Japanese and American history. In 1999, he published *Embracing Defeat,*[4] a study of the US postwar occupation of Japan. Turning again to popular culture, he detailed Japan's transition to democracy under US occupation, and the rapid reconstruction of Japan's devastated cities and people. *Embracing Defeat* was awarded the Pulitzer Prize for Nonfiction and the National Book Award for Nonfiction.

More recently, Dower has applied the same framework to his public criticism of both contemporary Japanese-US relations and of the US-led Iraq Wars* initiated in 1990 and 2003, with the presidential administration of George W. Bush* receiving particular scrutiny. Apparently, *Embracing Defeat* was required reading in Bush's cabinet. But Dower insists that it was misinterpreted and that, if they had read it properly, they would not have authorized the invasion and occupation of Iraq in 2003. Dower has drawn direct comparisons between the way the Bush administration politically constructed Muslims as inherently backwards and violent, and his analysis of Japanese-American relations during World War II. In his view, racist stereotyping has shaped the nature of violence in the Iraq conflicts just as it did between Japan and America in World War II.

In 2006, Dower received the John E. Thayer III Lifetime Achievement Award for his outstanding contributions to Japanese-American relations. Furthermore, Dower's broader argument linking popular culture, stereotypes, and violence—meaning his emphasis on the durable, replicative, and shifting patterns of racial thinking and practices—is now an important theme drawn on by many different disciplines across the social sciences (sociology and political science, for example).

NOTES

1   John W. Dower, *War Without Mercy: Race and Power in the Pacific War* (New York: Pantheon Books, 1993), 11.

2   Dower, *War Without Mercy,* 309.

3   Dower, *War Without Mercy,* 4.

4   John W. Dower, *Embracing Defeat: Japan in the Wake of World War II* (New York: W. W. Norton & Co., 1999).

SECTION 1
INFLUENCES

MODULE 1
THE AUTHOR AND THE HISTORICAL CONTEXT

KEY POINTS

- *War Without Mercy* is a detailed analysis of how popular culture generated the racial stereotypes which intensified the violence between the Americans and Japanese during World War II.*

- The author's training in Japanese-American history and his passion for cultural history* (a sub-field of history that uses culture to explain historical events) were the most significant factors that shaped his approach to the history of the Pacific War* (the battles fought in the Asia-Pacific region between 1941 and 1945).

- Dower wrote the book in the 1980s against a backdrop of the reemergence of political and economic tensions between the United States and Japan with both sides refashioning World War II stereotypes.

Why Read This Text?

Published in 1986, John Dower's *War Without Mercy* analyzes Japanese and American popular culture—music, film, popular writings, and cartoons—created during World War II. He reveals and questions shocking patterns of racial stereotypes that depicted both the Japanese and the American enemy as monkeys, insects, demons, and savages. The author argues that these dehumanized racial perceptions played an important role in shaping the atrocities committed by American and Japanese soldiers because the stereotypes created a psychological distancing from murder and made the extermination of the Other*

> **❝** Kill or be killed. No quarter, no surrender. Take no prisoners. Fight to the bitter end. These were everyday words in the combat areas, and in the final year of the war such attitudes contributed to an orgy of bloodletting that neither side could conceive of avoiding... **❞**
>
> John W. Dower, *War Without Mercy: Race and Power in the Pacific War*

(roughly, people who are emphatically "not us") desirable. Dower concludes that popular culture contributed significantly to creating a "war without mercy."

The book was written and published at a time when trans-Pacific relations had returned to the forefront of national imaginations in both the US and Japan. During the 1980s, economic and political tensions began to reemerge between the two countries. Dower saw that a number of reputable news outlets—including the *Washington Post*, the *Nation*, the *New Yorker* as well as *Asahi Jy naru* and *Asahi Shimbun*—were refashioning the racialized rhetoric employed during the Pacific War. As Dower wrote in 1986, "old and ominous attitudes have begun to reappear on both sides of the Pacific. The issue is race."[1]

War Without Mercy has contributed depth and nuance to the general understanding of Japanese-American relations during World War II. Moreover, Dower's approach to historical analysis, foregrounding the relationship between popular culture and the dehumanization and destruction of the Other, has influenced the continuing evolution of the social sciences.

Author's Life

John Dower was born in Providence, Rhode Island, in 1938. He completed a Bachelor of Arts degree in American studies at Amherst

College. He went on to Harvard University where he obtained a Master of Arts in East Asian studies and a doctorate in History and Far Eastern Language. Dower is a renowned historian of Japanese-American relations, and has written a number of important works on the subject. His best known contributions are *War Without Mercy* (1986) and *Embracing Defeat* (1999), both of which deal with the complexities of World War II and post-war dynamics between the United States and Japan.

Dower researched and taught for several years at the University of Nebraska-Lincoln and the University of Wisconsin-Madison, before moving on to the University of California, San Diego, where he worked as a professor until his retirement at the age of 72 in 2010. Currently, he is the Ford International Professor of History, Emeritus at the Massachusetts Institute of Technology (MIT). In this role, Professor Dower continues to contribute to the field of cultural history through "Visualizing Cultures," a web-based initiative launched in 2002 using a suite of visual materials to foster a deeper understanding of modern Japanese and Chinese history.

Dower has won several prestigious awards during the course of his career, including the National Book Award for Nonfiction, the Pulitzer Prize for General Nonfiction, and the Bancroft Prize. He was also the executive producer of the Academy Award-nominated documentary *Hellfire: A Journey from Hiroshima*, which illustrates how America's dropping of the atomic bomb has affected the Japanese people.

Author's Background

The methodology which Dower developed over the course of his career gave him a sharp insight into the return of racially dehumanizing language and imagery when, in the 1980s, a rivalry between Japan and the United States reignited, this time on the battlefield of the global economic markets. Again, inflammatory material came from both sides of the Pacific.[2] Dower highlighted remarks made by the Prime Minister of Japan, who said that Japanese racial purity accounted for their superior intelligence in comparison to that of the racially mixed peoples of the United States. This Japanese purity, he concluded, accounted for the manufacturing of superior products, giving rise to Japan's economic accomplishments.

Similarly, in the United States, Dower notes that by the mid-eighties both political figures and business leaders had fallen back into World War II racial rhetoric, representing the Japanese as aggressive "economic animals." The historical echo of the hostility coming from both opponents is exemplified by an example Dower cites of one American senator who labeled the increasing export of Japanese automobiles to the United States an "economic Pearl Harbor."*[3]

Dower's highlighting of racial rhetoric during the 1980s effectively supported his claims that racial stereotypes never disappear but, rather, shift and materialize in different conflicts and contexts. In this sense, Dower's articles, books, films, and digital initiatives in both the United States and Japan uncover important historical patterns in culture and conflict.

NOTES

1   John W. Dower, "Racial Slurs Hurt Relations between Japan and the West," *Ottawa Citizen*, October 11, 1986.

2   Dower, "Racial Slurs Hurt Relations between Japan and the West."

3   Dower, *War Without Mercy*, 313.

MODULE 2
ACADEMIC CONTEXT

KEY POINTS

- *War Without Mercy* explores the ways in which popular culture shaped racial stereotypes; these influenced the nature of the hostility between the Americans and Japanese during World War II.*

- This book is an important contribution to the sub-discipline of history known as cultural history*, which provides cultural explanations for historical experience.

- Dower's work contributes a nuanced perspective to our understanding of World War II Japanese-American relations as well as the shifting and durable nature of racism.

The Work in its Context

John Dower's *War Without Mercy* examines the important role racial hatred played in shaping the attitudes of the Americans and Japanese during World War II and the extreme violence in their military encounters. He bases his study on music, film, cartoons, and popular newspapers and magazines, and reveals shocking racial stereotypes. Dower argues that racism contributed to the brutality of the Pacific War* of 1941 to 1945.

3Placing popular culture at the center of his historical analysis, rather than relying solely on more official source material, Dower's approach subverted traditional historical methods. His work contributed to the sub-discipline of history known as cultural history, which provides cultural explanations for historical experiences. This sub-field began to develop in the 1960s and 1970s, and became more prominent in the 1980s when Dower published *War Without*

❝ As the traumatic events of World War II recede into the past, a new generation of historians, many of whom were born or educated after the war, are trying to analyze that monumental conflict in a more dispassionate way than has heretofore been possible. Impressed by the economic success and democratic stability of the former Axis powers, and disillusioned with the Cold War rhetoric of the present superpowers, these scholars have begun to reexamine what until recently have been considered axiomatic truths about that war. ❞

Ben-Ami Shillony,* "Review of *War Without Mercy: Race and Power in the Pacific War*"

Mercy. The text was one of the key early pieces of scholarship that examined popular culture in relation to Japan. In a 1989 interview, Dower explained that he was criticized for his decision to focus on film, music, and cartoons, "which many traditional historians would find too crude, and vulgar to qualify as 'serious' scholarship."[1] The author described his historical approach as an attempt to move beyond a narrow focus on national archives and the lives and decisions of government elites.

Overview of the Field

The core concept for *War Without Mercy*, as Dower recounts in the book's preface, occurred to him while he was working on another project about America's postwar occupation of Japan. He alluded to a link between the merciless fighting and hateful racist imagery, and realized that this connection, and the popular-culture subject matter through which these stereotypes were created and proliferated, were under-explored through conventional approaches to history.

Expanding this theory through research of both official sources and, most importantly, popular culture produced in America and Japan, Dower expanded the general understanding of the history of Japanese-US relations and also helped found the field of cultural history.

His early essays, articles, and other texts reveal the diversity of his influences and show the development of patterns in his research interests. His first book, *Elements of Japanese Design,*[2] is a compilation of 2,700 Japanese family crests with a lucid, thoroughly researched reflection on their changing uses and significance, from battlefield identification to symbols of familial pride and ancestry. Contemporary art took the central position in the 1980 publication *A Century of Japanese Photography,*[3] (which Dower edited) and in his essays "Japanese Artists and the Atomic Bomb,"[4] and "Art, Children and the Bomb."[5] These earlier texts reveal Dower's interest in cultural history, as well as in World War II-era Japan.

Dower was well positioned, as a cultural historian, to identify the connection between the popular racist perceptions of the enemy and the intense violence that took place during the Pacific War. Cultural history, however, was still an emerging field in the 1980s. Dower was one of the first historians to make use of cartoons, films, music, and popular writings to understand the history of Japan. In this regard, *War Without Mercy* helped revolutionize the contemporary approach to the study of history.

Academic Influences

Given Dower's interest in popular culture, and his resistance to traditional historical methods, it is unsurprising that he cites literature and art as his major influences. In particular, Dower mentions the poet and author Edgar Allan Poe[*] as someone who shaped his nature and ideas. Other major influences include the Japanese artists Iri and Toshi Maruki,[*] witnesses to the aftermath of the atomic bombing of Hiroshima,[*] who designed a series of murals depicting the devastation of the bomb on the Japanese people. The two artists later portrayed the heinous treatment of American prisoners of war in Japan as an acknowledgement of the atrocities committed by both sides of the conflict.

As a graduate student at Harvard University in 1969, John Dower was among the founding members of the Committee of Concerned Asian Scholars (CCAS),* a group of students and faculty at Harvard, Stanford University, the University of Michigan, the University of California at Berkeley, and Columbia University who promoted an end to the Vietnam War.* This political environment served as a catalyst for his interest in American foreign relations which, he states, eventually led to the writing of *War Without Mercy*.

As Dower mentions in an interview with the American news network C-Span, "I was very much drawn to cultural things … paintings, gardens, architecture." In the same interview, Dower explains that he made use of film and music, rather than formal documents, to understand the Japanese experience from the perspective of ordinary people.[6]

NOTES

1   Donna Olendorf et al., eds., *Contemporary Authors* (Detroit: Gale Research, 1992), 108–14.

2   John W. Dower, *The Elements of Japanese Design: A Handbook of Family Crests, Heraldry, and Symbolism* (New York: Weatherhill, 1971).

3   John W. Dower, ed., *A Century of Japanese Photography* (New York: Pantheon, 1980).

4   John W. Dower, "Japanese Artists and the Atomic Bomb," in John W. Dower, *Japan in War and Peace: Selected Essays* (New York: New Press, 1993), 242–56.

5   John W. Dower, "Art, Children and the Bomb," *Bulletin of Concerned Asian Scholars* 16, no. 2 (1984): 33-9.

6   John W. Dower, "Book Discussion: *Embracing Defeat*," C-Span, February 9, 2000, accessed June 9, 2015, http://www.c-span.org/video/?155311–1/book-discussion-embracing-defeat.

MODULE 3
THE PROBLEM

KEY POINTS

- Dower explores two core questions in this text: Why was the fighting between the Japanese and American soldiers so merciless and atrocious? And to what extent do stereotypes shape human behavior?

- Dower argues that popular culture played an essential role in shaping the brutality of American and Japanese violence during the war.

- By linking popular culture with stereotypes and violence, Dower's work makes an important and original contribution to our understanding of Japanese-American relations during World War II.*

Core Question

In the preface to *War Without Mercy*, John Dower explains the central questions guiding his study. First, Dower asks: Why was the fighting between Japanese and Americans in World War II so vicious, merciless, and atrocious? In answering this question, the author presents a novel understanding of the Japanese-American conflict. He argues that the Pacific War* of 1941 to 1945 was a racist war, and that popular culture provided the imagery which fueled this racism.

In conceptualizing the Pacific War as a racial conflict, Dower presents his second key question: How deeply can racial stereotypes influence human behavior? By analyzing Japanese and American music, film, popular writing, and cartoons, Dower concludes that racial stereotypes depicting the enemy as savage,

❝ What we are concerned with here is something different: the attachment of stupid, bestial, even pestilential subhuman caricatures on the enemy, and the manner in which this blocked seeing the foe as rational or even human, and facilitated mass killing. ❞

John Dower, *War Without Mercy: Race and Power in the Pacific War*

irrational, subhuman beasts created on both sides a psychological distance from the opponent and an obsession with exterminating the enemy.

On the surface, Dower's questions provide an important new analysis of the way racial stereotypes shaped the conflict between Japan and the United States. Its significance, however, exceeds the specific dynamics of Japanese-American relations as a result of Dower's remarkable uncovering of the pattern of racial stereotyping stretching back to the Spanish Inquisition* of the fifteenth century— an institution of the Catholic Church that demonized Jewish and Muslim people and executed many thousands of people accused of witchcraft. As Dower argues, the perception of the enemy as inferior and savage is a common recurring theme.

While focusing on the history of the Pacific War, Dower's perspective on this phenomenon expands the relevance of his insights beyond particular conflicts or countries, and across historical periods into the present day.

The Participants

To a great extent, *War Without Mercy* stands apart from mainstream scholarship on the Pacific War. Prior historical examinations by traditional Asian studies scholars relied heavily on American perceptions and source material, but largely excluded the views and voices of the Japanese. As some critics have noted, Dower's comparative study, which analyzes both American and Japanese sources, was an innovative contribution to World War II research. Since the publication of *War Without Mercy*, comparative analyses of the Pacific War have become the standard within this field.

The successful reception of the text should be seen against the backdrop of the development and growing popularity of cultural history* studies. A number of scholars, including Dower, helped further this development in the 1970s by calling for the inclusion of popular culture, including music and film, as a legitimate evidentiary base for historical argument. While the importance of popular culture may now seem obvious, at the time there was much debate over the significance of such sources in comparison with, for example, official documents from national archives. Dower's detailed analysis of Japanese and American racial stereotypes as portrayed in music and films, as well as in newspapers, magazines, and television cartoons, undeniably distinguishes him as a pioneering cultural historian.

The Contemporary Debate

War Without Mercy is a critically acclaimed contribution to the body of literature that attempts to present these alternative perspectives and approaches within Asian studies. In what has been termed the postmodern* wave of analysis, throughout the 1980s Dower and like-minded scholars were drawn to examinations of Asia, focusing on such themes as labor history, women's history, peasant revolts, folk culture, and other areas which, up to that point, had seldom featured in traditional histories. Rejecting history focused on grand narratives, monarchies and political leaders, scholars writing postmodern analyses produced works on "political, social and cultural activity peripheral to the centers of power."[1]

For historians with more traditional methods, Dower's source material was considered trivial. Examples of traditional works on Japan include The *Cambridge History of Japan,* a six-volume survey of Japanese history published by Cambridge University from 1988 to 1999 that aimed to present a comprehensive and authoritative historical picture from ancient Japan to the twentieth century. However, as Dower and many reviewers of the series concluded, "the Cambridge histories were themselves historical artefacts."[2] Critical reception noted the volumes' failure to address local history, women's history, personal histories, or any controversial history of social conflict. The *Cambridge History of Japan* focused instead on how political leaders shape history; the historical experience of ordinary Japanese was wholly missing. As Dower explained, "There's a whole neglected realm of activity … at the social and popular levels that's part of our history too and is very decisive, very influential."[3]

NOTES

1   John W. Dower, "Sizing Up (and Breaking Down) Japan," in Helen Hardacre, ed., *The Postwar Developments of Japanese Studies in the United States* (Leiden: E.J. Brill, 1998), 23.

2   Dower, "Sizing Up," 21.

3   Donna Olendorf et al., eds., *Contemporary Authors* (Detroit: Gale Research, 1992), 108–14.

MODULE 4
THE AUTHOR'S CONTRIBUTION

KEY POINTS

- John Dower showed how popular culture in the United States and Japan shaped racial stereotypes, and linked dehumanizing stereotyping to the scale of the violence against the enemy in World War II.*

- This approach, which told the story of Japanese-American World War II relations from a popular perspective, helped fuel the development of the sub-field of cultural history,* which examined historical questions through the lens of popular culture.

- Dower's argument linking popular culture to the violent behavior of the Americans and Japanese during the Pacific War* provided the first comprehensive study of racism within World War II history scholarship.

Author's Aims

John Dower's *War Without Mercy* was intended to address two audiences: academics in the field of Japanese and American relations, and a general readership of those interested in history and politics, particularly World War II. Judging by the numerous positive reviews in academic journals and popular newspapers, as well as the awards the author received, the text succeeded in reaching both of these audiences.

The author sought to break away from a traditional approach to US scholarship on World War II that generally told the story only from the American perspective. By drawing his arguments and conclusions from popular culture sources in the United States

❝ Prejudice and racial stereotypes frequently distorted both Japanese and Allied evaluations of the enemy's intentions and capabilities. Race hate fed atrocities, and atrocities in turn fanned the fires of race hate.**❞**

John Dower, *War Without Mercy: Race and Power in the Pacific War*

and Japan, Dower was able to achieve this objective by presenting a more balanced account of Japanese-American relations that his predecessors. Ultimately, he found that popular culture in both countries had shaped stereotypes of the enemy as subhuman, granting both the Americans and the Japanese the psychological distance necessary to commit extreme atrocities.

Dower's focus on popular culture ran contrary to the dominant trend in scholarly research that concentrated on archival research and political leaders. While some traditional historians questioned the seriousness of analyzing "low culture" sources like movies, magazines, and cartoons, this innovative approach proved profoundly revealing and contributed significantly to the history of the Pacific War and to contemporary methodologies within the social sciences.

Approach

Dower decided to research the core theme in the text after writing a sentence in a manuscript on a planned book about the American occupation of Japan following World War II. In the opening paragraph of the manuscript, Dower spoke of how merciless and racially charged the conflict between Americans and Japanese had been. He then remarked that despite the brutality of the Pacific War, the racial hatred between Americans and Japanese seemed to disappear overnight following the end of the conflict.

As Dower states in the text, the question of how bitter racial hatred could transform so easily and quickly into positive cooperation between Japan and the United States was mind-boggling. It was Dower's curiosity about the sudden shift that sparked a research project that culminated in his seminal work *War Without Mercy*. Drawing on music, films, popular writings, and cartoons, with material from both sides of the Pacific, Dower compares the effects of racial stereotypes on Japanese and American military strategy, planning, and conduct. As Dower argues, popular racial stereotypes portraying the Japanese and American enemy as beasts, savages, and subhuman animals directly influenced the merciless, "take no prisoners" nature of the bloodthirsty battles between the two sides in the Pacific.

Contribution in Context

In answering the paradoxical question of why Japanese-American relations were so racially charged and brutal during World War II, and so cooperative almost immediately after Japan's surrender, Dower expands into his larger argument, making an important contribution to the social sciences and cultural studies.

Dower employs the popular anthropological and philosophical concept of the Self and the Other* to scrutinize the evolution of racism since the Spanish Inquisition* in the fifteenth century. The Other is a person or a thing that is defined as different from oneself. This difference informs one's own identity. According to this model, we only have a self-identity in opposition to what we are not. This perspective on identity as formed by what the Self excludes (that is, the Other) is now a well-established method of social-scientific inquiry. A number of scholars, among them the Palestinian American literary theorist Edward Said,* have focused on how popular culture contributes to shaping an image of a particular group as backwards and subhuman, which in turn serves as a pretext for imperialism* and violence.

Dower argues that racial stereotypes do not disappear after

conflicts cease, but instead transfer onto new enemies. The change in cultural representations from the end of World War II to the beginning of the Cold War* (a period of tension between the Soviet Union and its allies and the US and its allies that began after World War II and ended with the collapse of the Soviet Union in 1991) perfectly demonstrates this shift. As Dower explains briefly, Japan and the United States, who were once bitter enemies, quickly created a shared identity through their new communist* enemies. The Japanese Other became part of the American Self, and the racial language of World War II was used to describe the new enemy Other: the Soviet Union.

SECTION 2
IDEAS

MODULE 5
MAIN IDEAS

KEY POINTS

- The central idea of the text is that popular culture created and popularized racial stereotypes which stoked the violence between the Americans and the Japanese during World War II.*

- Dower's broader thesis is that racism is a phenomenon that can shift onto new subjects but is durable over time.

- The author presents this main idea in highly descriptive language that has a powerful and persuasive impact on the reader.

Key Themes

John Dower's methodology in *War Without Mercy* centers on the crucial interrelation between the Self and the Other.* This is a dichotomy—an oppositional pairing—of long standing in the social sciences, popularized in the literary theorist Edward Said's* seminal 1978 text *Orientalism*. Said positioned the Self as corresponding to the occident (the West) and the Other as aligned with the orient (the East).[1] The basic idea is that individuals only have an identity in opposition to what they are not.

During the Pacific War* the Americans and the Japanese came to see themselves as the opposite of one another. The Americans viewed themselves as civilized in contrast to the savagery of the Japanese, and the Japanese saw themselves as virtuous and racially "pure" in contrast to America's racial adulteration and beastliness.

This Self-Other concept can be deployed to analyze the construction of local or national identity in a number of other

> ❝ Upon closer examination ... these portraits of the enemy reveal that stereotypes operated several ways in the war between Japan and the Anglo-American powers. First, they followed predictable patterns of contrariness in which each side portrayed the other as its polar opposite: as darkness opposed to its own radiant light. Second, the positive self-images of one side were singled out for ridicule and condemnation by the other. Self-stereotypes fed hostile stereotypes...❞
>
> John Dower, *War Without Mercy: Race and Power in the Pacific War*

historical contexts. For example, French city-dwellers in the nineteenth and twentieth centuries viewed themselves as the polar opposite of rural peasants: that is, they saw themselves as urban, industrial, and sophisticated in contrast to agricultural workers, who they perceived as backwards and uncivilized.

Influenced by this concept, in *War Without Mercy* Dower argued that American and Japanese popular culture created and defined stereotypes of their respective enemy as someone who was unworthy of mercy. To the Japanese, the American enemies were devils, demons, or simply deranged. For Americans, the Japanese enemies were primitive apes and irrational madmen. The result on both sides of this dehumanization of the Other was a psychological distancing that permitted the vicious killing of unarmed prisoners, the desecration of the dead, and a vicious obsession with exterminating the enemy.

Exploring the Ideas

Among the questions raised, Dower grapples with these: first, why was the battle between Americans and Japanese during World War II so much more savage than the conflict between

Americans and the European Axis powers* (Nazi Germany and Fascist Italy)? And second, why did Americans and Japanese hate each other so passionately?

Turning to the music, movies, cartoons, and popular writing of the war era, Dower uncovers a striking pattern. Racial stereotypes of the enemy flooded popular culture on both sides of the Pacific. The enemy was depicted as irrational, barbaric, and, ultimately, unworthy of life. Dower argued that these widespread racist values and images of the enemy provoked such atrocious war behavior as the killing of unarmed prisoners, and most controversially, America's dropping of the atomic bomb over Hiroshima* and Nagasaki*.

Where Americans represented themselves as the model of rationality and civilization, the Japanese were portrayed as irrational savages. In Japan, their nation was represented as pure and moral, while Americans were depicted as demons and impure beasts. Fitting seamlessly into the concept of the Self and the Other, both Japanese and American racial stereotypes relied necessarily on their own self-image as the polar opposite of their enemy Other. As Dower writes, this dangerous psychological distancing induced the same results for Japan and the US, "an obsession with extermination on both sides—a war without mercy."[2]

While *War Without Mercy* certainly provides a pioneering approach to its subject and unique insights into the nature of culture and military hostility, it is necessary to maintain a critical approach to Dower's central argument. Some scholars have accused him of overemphasizing the power of media and popular culture. Notably missing from Dower's text are any accounts of Americans or Japanese resisting the blatant racial stereotypes surrounding them, although political rhetoric and propaganda are never accepted unanimously. The absence of such voices in Dower's study could lead the reader to believe that everyone in the population readily accepted the virulent racial stereotypes of the enemy Other.

Language and Expression

Since Dower draws his findings from popular culture, his language is highly descriptive. His central thesis revolves around the idea that words and images shape people's behavior, even those based on completely irrational stereotypes. If they are propagated in a certain way with a high degree of repetition, they have the power to convince people to do barbaric things outside their normal moral framework. His description of American soldiers sending the dismembered body parts of Japanese casualties back home to their wives serves as a particularly disturbing example.

Throughout the book, the dialectic of the Self and the Other frames Dower's line of thinking. While, as mentioned above, Dower wasn't the originator of this notion, the author was the first historian to apply it as a way of furthering our understanding of Japanese-American relations and racism during World War II. This concept again highlights the power of language and images in convincing people that an opposing group is subhuman and deserves to suffer violence and even death.

Dower's writing style is confident and engaging, with clear descriptive passages, convincing argument, and a sense of involvement with the visual material on which he bases his conclusions. The balance of facts and analysis, along with an approachable narrative tone, make the book accessible to academics and a general audience alike.

NOTES

1   Edward Said, *Orientalism* (London: Routledge & Kegan Paul, 1978).

2   John W. Dower, *War Without Mercy: Race and Power in the Pacific War* (New York: Pantheon Books, 1993), 11.

MODULE 6
SECONDARY IDEAS

KEY POINTS

- A key secondary idea in the text is the parallel the author draws between stereotyping and violence in fifteenth-century Spain and that which occurred during World War II.*

- This idea supports the author's broader point that racism is a malleable and durable concept—it can take many forms, and it endures.

- An often overlooked secondary assertion is the extent to which racist ideology informed the large-scale internment of Japanese Americans and the US decision to drop atomic bombs over Hiroshima* and Nagasaki.*

Other Ideas

A key secondary idea in John Dower's *War Without Mercy* is that the construction of racial stereotypes as a tool of warfare is not unique to the conflict between the United States and Japan. Rather, the racist language that fueled World War II reflects a similar pattern of conflicts between the racially normative and those racialized-as-Other* dating back to fifteenth-century Spain.

Tracing a pattern of racial language to the Spanish Conquest of indigenous peoples in the Americas and in the Spanish Inquisition* in Europe, Dower argues that the racial stereotypes of the Pacific War* emerged from a heritage of slavery and colonial racial language. As Dower analyzes this connection, he finds that the American popular perception of the Japanese as irrational, savage, inferior human beings had long been used to describe the encounters and

❝ There was a free-floating quality to portrayals of the enemy, a pattern of stereotyping peculiar to enemies and "others" in general, rather than to the Japanese foe or Western foe in particular. This facilitated the quick abatement of hatred once the war had ended—while also facilitating the transferal of the hateful stereotypes to newly perceived enemies. Much of the rhetoric of World War II proved readily adaptable to the Cold War. ❞

John Dower, *War Without Mercy: Race and Power in the Pacific War*

conflicts between white and non-white peoples. Just as these racial stereotypes legitimized the colonization of the New World and the decimation of indigenous Americans by Spanish conquistadors and other European colonial powers, Dower argues, this same racial language facilitated such atrocities as the killing of unarmed Japanese prisoners, and the aerial bombing of civilian targets.

Dower clearly sees racism as a tool to justify and promote the achievement of one group's imperial* ambitions—that is, the drive to build an empire—through dominating another group.

Exploring the Ideas

At various points in *War Without Mercy,* Dower provides a textual comparison to demonstrate the durability and adaptability of racial stereotyping within transnational conflicts. To this end, he presents quotes separated from the body text. Some of the quotations are contemporary to the Pacific War while some derive from fifteenth-century Spain, but Dower omits the sources, inviting the reader to distinguish fifteenth-century rhetoric from that of the twentieth century. This is almost impossible, however, as similar terms such as "barbarian," "savage," "inferior," "child," and "beast" appear in works written nearly four centuries apart. This exercise by Dower stands as a powerful reinforcement for his argument of the long pattern and durability of racial stereotyping.

In concluding his text, Dower points to the greater significance of this pattern of racial language, not only leaving the reader with instances of this pattern's early incarnations, but also its present and its potential future. As Dower states, these racial stereotypes do not disappear after conflicts cease, but instead become the terms that are used to describe new enemies. By the 1950s, the Japanese were no longer seen as savages in the American imagination; they were viewed as allies and friends. America's new communist* enemies, however, quickly became savages and barbarians. Written in 1986, the text's usefulness in understanding the Cold War* hatred between Americans and Russians is quite effective.

War Without Mercy was also timely because it linked the language and imagery of the 1940s with the Japanese-American trade tensions of the 1980s. As Dower made clear, in the midst of the rising Japanese and American political-economic conflict of the 1980s, the racial language of World War II was making an ominous reappearance in speeches made by American and Japanese officials and business leaders. This highlights both the malleability and durability of racism over time.

Overlooked

Dower's text represents a significant and lasting contribution to Japanese history, as well as the emerging field of cultural history.* However, there are significant areas of *War Without Mercy* that are worthy of further consideration and elaboration. For example, in addition to the atrocities committed by Japanese and American soldiers, Dower argues that racial stereotypes influenced misguided military intelligence and strategy, and that "such dehumanization … surely facilitated the decisions to make civilian populations the targets of concentrated attack, whether by conventional or nuclear weapons."[1] In essence, Dower is arguing that the Americans' decision to drop atomic bombs over Hiroshima and Nagasaki was not only misguided but motivated by racist stereotypes propagated by popular culture. This interpretation was controversial at the time of the book's publication in 1986, and remains so more than two decades later. However, only a relatively small proportion of the text is devoted to this momentous topic, touching on the subject just twice in 11 chapters and leaving some critics to wonder whether such a weighty assertion on the nature of one of the most fateful events in human history deserves further attention.

Another area of *War Without Mercy* that could merit further examination is the idea that the US internment of more than 110,000 people of Japanese ancestry was an example of anti-Japanese racism in the United States. He presents a compelling argument that racial stigmatization of the Japanese was the cause, as no comparable action was taken against people of German or Italian origins. However, much like his argument of the racial motivations behind the use of the atomic bomb, the topic of Japanese internment received little attention in the text and could have illustrated his position in greater detail.

One further limitation of the study is the author's lack of comparison between American-Japanese atrocities in World War II and hostility between Americans and the European Axis* powers (Nazi Germany and Fascist Italy). A comparative reference to the Holocaust* (the genocide of Jewish people in Europe during World War II) as an example of racial violence in the context of the Self and the Other would seem logical but does not appear in *War Without Mercy*.

NOTES

1   John W. Dower, *War Without Mercy: Race and Power in the Pacific War* (New York: Pantheon Books, 1993), 11.

MODULE 7
ACHIEVEMENT

KEY POINTS

- Dower illuminates the extent to which racist stereotypes propelled the violence between the Americans and the Japanese in World War II.*

- The balanced use of sources of popular culture from both America and Japan successfully avoided the conventional bias toward an American point of view. This comparative focus has brought Dower great acclaim on both sides of the Pacific.

- Although *War Without Mercy* is an essential text, the book does possess some limitations, including areas where comparisons with other fronts of the war could have strengthened its argument.

Assessing the Argument

In *War Without Mercy*, John Dower argues that American and Japanese popular culture during World War II contributed greatly to the brutal violence that occurred between the two sides. Text and images in newspapers, film, and music portrayed the Other* as subhuman and encouraged its extermination. The author argues that this shaped the atrocities that took place, including the mistreatment of prisoners of war, the murder of surrendering troops, and perhaps most controversially, the dropping of the atomic bomb. As Dower puts it: "In countless ways, war words and race words came together in a manner which did not just reflect the savagery of the war, but contributed to it by reinforcing the impression of a truly Manichean* struggle between completely incompatible antagonists. The natural response to such a vision was an

66 Employing a variety of sources, from official documents to cartoons, movies, songs, and advertisements, the author presents us with a beautifully written and nicely illustrated book. It is also, however, a deeply depressing one, in that it portrays the record of narrow-mindedness, bigotry, inhumanity, and sheer human folly that accompanied the war on both sides of the Pacific. 99

Ben-Ami Shillony,* "Review of *War Without Mercy: Race and Power in the Pacific War*"

obsession with extermination on both sides—war without mercy."[1] ("Manichean" here refers to the, supposedly, perfectly contrasting natures of the "antagonists," the US and Japan.)

Dower's study has been seen by some[2] as a relatively balanced presentation of racism. Drawing his findings from an array of popular culture sources in Japan and the United States, he argues that this phenomenon was equally prevalent on both sides.

Dower published the book, in English and in Japanese, to a positive reception in both countries, winning the National Book Critics Circle Award in the US and the Japanese Masayoshi Ohira Memorial Prize for distinguished studies of the Pacific Basin Community, among other accolades. Since publication, the work has become an important point of reference for understanding wartime Japanese-American relations, as well as providing reflections of historical movements within popular culture and the racialization of rival groups.

Achievement in Context

Dower is widely regarded as one of the foremost historians of Japanese-American history. The author's use of popular culture to describe racism during World War II was an original contribution to history and the social sciences. Moreover, *War Without Mercy* powerfully and persuasively explains how racial stereotypes prevalent in the Pacific conflict did not disappear but, rather, were redirected towards other enemies—as was the case when the US began to portray the Soviet Union (an ally during World War II) as "the Evil Empire" during the Cold War,* and indeed vice versa.

Dower also describes how, after Japan lost the war, it become an ally of the US in its struggle against communism.* It was as if, overnight, the mutual Otherness that characterized the dynamic of World War II had disappeared. This is in part because the cessation of the fighting made it unnecessary, and also because defeated Japan was now occupied by the US military and required its protection, following the loss of its own armed forces. As Dower puts it: "To the victors, the simian became a pet … Victory confirmed the Allies' assumption of superiority, while the ideology of a 'proper place' enabled the Japanese to adjust to being a good loser. Even the demonic Other … posed no obstacle to the transition from enmity to amicable relations as Japan quickly moved under the US military aegis."[3]

The Japanese had little choice but to become a US ally if it wanted to rebuild economically and be protected militarily in the aftermath of World War II, and the US had a new enemy—Soviet communism—to target as the Other.

Limitations

Like most books advancing unconventional methods or interpretations, *War Without Mercy* has received criticism ranging from the trivial to the more relevant and consequential. One reviewer questioned the very premise implied within the book's title, asking if there could be such a thing as a *merciful* war? Was the war in the Pacific really more savage than the war in Europe? It is possible to find the answer to the first question within the multiple examples Dower offers of what constituted Japanese and American atrocities beyond the violence normally associated with war. A merciful war would be one in which prisoners of war were not executed, body parts of the enemy were not collected as souvenirs, and civilian populations were not targeted by military forces. The reviewer's second question, however, points to a significant absence in Dower's text. Few comparisons are drawn between the European and Pacific theaters of World War II, leaving the reader to simply take Dower at his word that the combatants in the US-Japanese battle were far less respectful of established military rules of engagement.

This criticism is not entirely valid, however, as Dower does intimate that although Americans saw the Germans as the enemy on the war's European fronts, they still regarded them as part of the "white race," whereas the Japanese were portrayed as a non-white, non-human, sub-category. In making this point, Dower quotes George Washington,* the first American president, who called Native Americans "beasts," the 26th American president, Theodore Roosevelt,* who claimed that a good Indian was a dead Indian, and the historian Henry Adams* who stated that "the Japs are monkeys."[4] As the author puts it, "What we are concerned with here is … the attachment of stupid, bestial, even pestilential subhuman caricatures on the enemy, and the manner in which this blocked seeing the foe as rational or even human, and facilitated mass killing."[5]

NOTES

1   John W. Dower, *War Without Mercy: Race and Power in the Pacific War* (New York: Pantheon Books, 1993), 11.

2   See, for example: Ben-Ami Shillony, "Review: War Without Mercy: Race and Power in the Pacific War by John W. Dower," *Journal of Japanese Studies* 14, no. 1 (1988): 200–5.

3   Dower, *War Without Mercy*, 13.

4   Cited in Shillony, "Review: War Without Mercy," 200–5.

5   Dower, *War Without Mercy*, 98.

MODULE 8
PLACE IN THE AUTHOR'S WORK

KEY POINTS

- Dower has produced a coherent corpus on racism within the context of Japanese-American relations. This has consisted of books, journal and press articles, a documentary, and a web-based visual history project.

- *War Without Mercy* and *Embracing Defeat* are Dower's most important works.

- Dower's corpus has highlighted the importance of popular culture and its potential to shape stereotyping and violence.

Positioning

When John Dower published *War Without Mercy* in 1986, he had already been an associate professor of history at the University of Nebraska-Lincoln for eight years, a professor of history at the University of Wisconsin-Madison for six years, and had just begun a professorship at the University of California-San Diego. Furthermore, Dower had served as an editor for three texts dealing with Japanese history, and he had written two important books: *The Elements of Japanese Design* (1971)[1] and *Empire and Aftermath* (1979).[2]

From graduate school through his multiple professorships, Dower published 25 articles on Japanese history in both English and Japanese publications, as well as press articles in the *New York Times*, the *Washington Post*, and Japan's largest daily newspaper, the *Yomiuri Shimbun*. *War Without Mercy* represented the work of a mature and extensively published historian. This is evident in the depth of Dower's argument, and his use of popular culture to

❝ Whether we read this book from the American, Japanese, or a third party point of view, it will help us exorcise the demon of racism that has bedeviled human society for a very long time. **❞**

Ben-Ami Shillony,* "Review of *War Without Mercy: Race and Power in the Pacific War*"

recount a detailed story of Japanese-American relations during World War II*—a novel approach that required significant training and expertise to successfully reach two distinct audiences, American and Japanese.

Integration

Following *War Without Mercy*, Dower published a book of selected essays titled *Japan in War and Peace* (1993).[3] Similar to *War Without Mercy*, these essays deal with racial stereotypes and attitudes relying upon a similar evidentiary basis of film, music, and visual art. In essence, *Japan in War and Peace* expands upon Dower's earlier interests in Japanese racial stereotypes through an analysis of racial effects in wartime, postwar, and contemporary Japan. Dower's usage of the concept of the Self and the Other* in *War Without Mercy* is similarly deployed in chapter nine of the text, "Graphic Others/ Graphic Selves: Cartoon in War and Peace."

Dower's most celebrated book, however, is his 1999 work, *Embracing Defeat*.[4] Picking up largely where *War Without Mercy* concluded, *Embracing Defeat* examines America's postwar occupation of Japan from 1945 to 1952. Focusing on the Japanese narrative, Dower again relies on sources of popular culture to examine racial stereotypes, but also pays due attention to the political dynamics of occupied Japan. *Embracing Defeat* was awarded numerous prizes, including the National Book Award for Nonfiction, the Pulitzer Prize for General Nonfiction, and the Bancroft Prize from Columbia University.

These two books, along with Dower's wider corpus, have cemented his legacy as one of the foremost experts on Japanese-American history and relations.

Significance

Dower's body of work is varied. His achievements include several book and journal articles, press contributions, the 1986 Academy Award-nominated documentary *Hellfire*—which explores the art of Japanese depictions of the atomic bomb—as well as the ongoing digital web-project "Visualizing Cultures" at MIT that combines graphic materials with original, critical analyses by Dower on the history of modern Japan and China. Dower's body of work continues to grow; his most notable recent publication is *Cultures of War* (2011).

All of these contributions link popular culture with Asian history and form a coherent corpus. Dower has profoundly illuminated the role of racism in World War II Japanese-American relations, an aspect of the conflict that had largely been ignored prior to his analysis. His powerful words and visual depictions have fostered a greater consciousness of the phenomenon of dehumanization and military aggression.

More recently, Dower has become a vocal critic of American imperialism*—policy of empire building—in other parts of the world. For example, in 1991 he wrote an article in which he criticized American foreign policy in the Gulf War,* fought for six months over 1990 and 1991. In another piece, "Japan and the US Samurai Spirit,"[5] he drew convincing parallels between the aggressive war policies of the United States towards Iraq with the "war-loving, ultra-nationalistic"* foreign policies of Japan in the 1930s and 1940s.[6] Furthermore, in 1995, Dower voiced his criticism of the US Senate's decision to denounce a forthcoming exhibition at the National Air and Space Museum in Washington that was to feature a poster that criticized America's dropping of the atomic bomb on Hiroshima* and Nagasaki.* The US Congress threatened to cut federal funding to the museum for what they viewed as offensive and revisionist questioning of the decision to use atomic weapons (here, "revisionist" refers to a perceived attempt to change a long-accepted interpretation of historical events). Opponents of the exhibit argued that proposed material did not discuss the ferocity and atrocious war behavior of the Japanese. Dower agreed with this criticism, but added the argument he made in *War Without Mercy*: the Americans were also guilty of ferociousness and war atrocities, and the dropping of the atomic bomb was driven by America's racial hatred of the Japanese.[7] The planned exhibit was eventually canceled, and the director of the museum resigned over the controversy. Today, Dower continues to be a vocal critic of racism, violence, and imperialism.

NOTES

1   John W. Dower, *The Elements of Japanese Design: A Handbook of Family Crests, Heraldry, and Symbolism* (New York: Weatherhill, 1971).

2   John W. Dower, *Empire and Aftermath: Yoshida Shigeru and the Japanese Experience* (Cambridge: Harvard University Press, 1979).

3   John W. Dower, *Japan in War and Peace: Selected Essays* (New York: New Press, 1993).

4   John W. Dower, *Embracing Defeat: Japan in the Wake of World War II* (New York: W.W. Norton & Co., 1999).

5   John W. Dower, "Japan and the US Samurai Spirit," *Bulletin of the Atomic Scientists* 47, no. 5 (1991): 29–30.

6   Dower, "Japan and the US Samurai Spirit": 28.

7   John W. Dower, "Triumphal and Tragic Narratives of the War in Asia," *Journal of American History* 82, no. 3 (1995): 1129.

SECTION 3
IMPACT

MODULE 9
THE FIRST RESPONSES

KEY POINTS

- The most prominent criticism Dower received for *War Without Mercy* is that he focused too much on American racism and too little on that of the Japanese.

- Another important criticism is that Dower gives too much primacy to racial stereotypes in explaining violence and does not account for other possible causes or motivating factors.

- Although the author has made minor modifications to his argument, it has remained largely consistent over time.

Criticism

On publication, John Dower's *War Without Mercy* received wide recognition and praise, including the National Book Critics Circle Award in General Nonfiction. The text set a standard for scholarship on Japanese-American relations during World War II* against which current work is still benchmarked and compared.

Critics have rightly pointed out the disparity between the amount of attention given to American racial stereotypes of the Japanese, and Japanese racial stereotypes of Americans. Although remarkably nonpartisan, *War Without Mercy* does indeed devote more space to the racist American portrayals of the Japanese. This could be due to lack of Japanese source material, much of which, Dower noted, was lost in multiple fires caused by the American nuclear assault prior to Japan's surrender.

War Without Mercy is revisionist, however, in posing a challenge to long-accepted understandings of historical events. Dower consciously

> **❝The armed conflict in the Pacific was a race war, powered by mutual hatreds and stereotyping.❞**
> Ronald Takaki,* *Double Victory: A Multicultural History of America in World War II*

attempts to reverse the dominant view that war atrocities, such as the inhumane treatment of soldiers, were committed solely by the Japanese. This may account for the slight bias in Dower's analysis.

Most persuasive, however, is the argument that Dower overemphasized the power of media and propaganda. These critics suggest that the transmission of ideas by way of movies, music, newspapers, and magazines never provides a complete picture. In effect, *War Without Mercy* is criticized for not offering counterpoints to those consumed by racial hatred of the Japanese or American enemy. These "voices of reason," as one critic labeled them, would display the capacity of people to think critically even in the worst of times.[1] This criticism is the most justifiable concern of Dower's text, since it is unreasonable to assume there was no opposition to the blatant racism promoted throughout Japanese and American popular culture. However, even the critics who pointed out these omissions and imbalances recognize the significance and value of Dower's main thesis that the Japanese and American conflict must be understood as "a racial war."

Responses

Following *War Without Mercy,* Dower's essay "Race, Language, and War in Two Cultures" has been frequently reprinted in historical readers and collections of essays pertaining to World War II. In it, Dower recapitulates the main thesis and ideas of *War Without Mercy* that the popular, dehumanizing rhetoric of Japanese and American enemies generated racial stereotypes that promoted gratuitous violence in the Pacific.

While the main arguments of *War Without Mercy* are largely unaltered in this essay, in several instances Dower appears to respond to comments raised by his critics. For example, in the introduction of "Race, Language, and War in Two Cultures," Dower concedes: "World War II in Asia was, of course, not simply or even primarily a race war. Alliances cut across race on both the Allied and Axis sides, and fundamental issues of power and ideology were at stake."[2] Although Dower never explicitly states that racism fully accounts for every heinous action in the Pacific War,* he also does not offer the reader any alternative causes.

The small but telling concessions Dower makes in "Race, Language, and War in Two Cultures," suggests a dialogue with the critiques of *War Without Mercy*. However, the fundamental arguments of the text have remained unmodified through four reprints of this essay, the most recent of which, to date, was published in 2012. For Dower, race continues to be a highly significant lens through which one can understand the Japanese–American conflict in World War II.

Conflict and Consensus

Published over two decades ago, *War Without Mercy* remains seminal. As Dower wrote, racism was previously "a neglected aspect of World War II."[3] Following Dower's introduction of racism into the analysis of the Pacific War, a multitude of studies centering on race and its influences during the war era have been published. Subsequent historians influenced by Dower have extended and elaborated the arguments of *War Without Mercy* in the decades following its publication.

In *Hiroshima: Why America Dropped the Atomic Bomb* (1995), Ronald Takaki furthers one of Dower's most controversial arguments in *War Without Mercy* by arguing that the US decision to drop the atomic bomb on Hiroshima* and Nagasaki* was influenced by the prevalent anti–Japanese racism. As Takaki writes: "In Europe the enemy was identified as [Adolf] Hitler* and the Nazis,* not the German people. In the Pacific ... American anger was generally aimed at an entire people, the 'Japs'."[4] In his view, an American populace that conflated the Japanese enemy with the Japanese people accepted the mass annihilation of Japanese civilians.

Others, among them the specialist on Asian-American history Roger Daniels* and the cultural historian Allan Austin,* have found significant utility in Dower's remarks on the link between racism and the internment of people of Japanese ancestry in the United States. By developing this less-central aspect of Dower's analysis, scholars have expanded his argument, underscoring the inherent racism behind the mass incarceration of Japanese Americans, particularly in light of the fact that no similar policy was perpetrated against people of German or Italian ancestry. The perception of racial difference, these critics suggest, informed a distinctly separate treatment of different opponents by the US.

NOTES

1   David Lu, "Review: War Without Mercy," *The Journal of Asian Studies* 46, no. 4 (1987).

2   John W. Dower, "Race, Language and War," in John W. Dower, ed., *Japan in War and Peace: Selected Essays* (New York: New Press, 1994).

3   John W. Dower, *War Without Mercy: Race and Power in the Pacific War* (New York: Pantheon Books, 1993), 4.

4   Ronald Takaki, *Hiroshima: Why America Dropped the Atomic Bomb* (Boston: Back Bay Books, 1996), 8.

MODULE 10
THE EVOLVING DEBATE

KEY POINTS

- The text was the first major work in cultural history* on Japanese-American World War II* relations.

- *War Without Mercy* has had a broad and enduring impact on our understanding of Japanese-American history and racism.

- The text has served as a foundation for further research on these subjects, and studies of popular culture more broadly.

Uses and Problems

John Dower's *War Without Mercy* has had a wide-ranging and lasting influence. Dower's early interest in literature and art, combined with his training in American studies as an undergraduate at Amherst College, positioned him as an early adopter and pioneering practitioner of the emerging field of cultural history. *War Without Mercy* represented the first comparative analysis of World War II popular culture that included Japan. Dower's study of magazines, films, music, cartoons, and popular writings has influenced subsequent generations of historians to take seriously the importance of popular culture in historical inquiry.

By arguing that racial stereotypes depicted in American and Japanese popular culture influenced military conduct in the Pacific War,* Dower contributed a groundbreaking reinterpretation of World War II. Dower's approach is interdisciplinary, drawing on the methods and aims of different academic fields; this, with the book's focus on popular culture and its balance of cultural material

"Race hate fed atrocities, and atrocities in turn fanned the fire of race hate."

John Dower, *War Without Mercy: Race and Power in the Pacific War*

from both America and Japan, has earned *War Without Mercy* wide popularity and influence beyond the field of history.

Unsurprisingly, given Dower's engagement with Japanese and American movies, numerous scholars in film studies have engaged with the central arguments of the text. In analyzing the 2006 American movie *Letters From Iwo Jima*, the cultural historian and film critic Leo Braudy* praises the cinematography and unbiased approach of the movie in its treatment of both American and Japanese soldiers. As Braudy argues, American movies have tended to cast the Japanese as incorrigibly evil. *Letters from Iwo Jima* builds on Dower's comparative approach by utilizing documents from both American and Japanese soldiers to build its narrative.[1] Other scholars in film studies have extended Dower's analysis to examinations of the racial portrayals of the Vietnamese in American films of the Vietnam War,* while many have applied similar methods to the interpretation of the World War II newsreels and propaganda films Dower details in *War Without Mercy*.

Nina Cornyetz,* a scholar of gender and sexuality, uses *War Without Mercy* to scrutinize the modern Japanese fetishizing of African American style. As Cornyetz details, in the 1990s young Japanese men began adopting the style of hip-hop culture in the United States, including baggy pants and expensive shoes, with some going so far as to darken their faces with makeup. According to Cornyetz, the impure and polluted racial image that Dower had presented as Japan's dominant perception of Americans had been reversed by the 1990s. Arguing that the US post-war occupation of Japan had feminized the nation, Cornyetz states that young Japanese men have turned to the style of African Americans to signify masculinity and power.[2]

Schools of Thought

In *War Without Mercy*, John Dower integrated the historical study of traditional primary sources, such as government documents, with non-traditional sources like films, music, cartoons, and popular writings. As he explained in 2012, his objective was to meld the voices of the elite with the experiences of typical Japanese and American people living during the conflict.[3] Cultural history was then an emerging practice for scholarship in the European and American academic field and *War Without Mercy* represented the first significant mark of popular culture in the study of Asian history. The effects of Dower's pioneering investigation have reverberated throughout subsequent histories of Japanese and American relations.

The historian Roger Daniels,* for example, has related anti-Japanese racism to the motivations behind the US internment of Japanese Americans during the war. As Daniels writes, "the broad historical causes which shaped these decisions were race prejudice, war hysteria, and a failure of political leadership."[4] Daniels details the coverage of false stories reporting espionage by people of Japanese ancestry in American press and radio. However, throughout the duration of the war, not a single case of sabotage was committed by a Japanese or Japanese American person living in the United States.

In his 2011 article "Superman Goes to War," the cultural historian Allan Austin* offers a similar interpretation of the decision behind Japanese internment. Analyzing a popular episode of the *Superman* comic, Austin uncovers racial stereotypes presenting Japanese Americans as untrustworthy, corrupt, and evil.[5] Austin argues that this cartoon displays the common conflation of the Japanese enemy with all Japanese, and contributed to the popular support of mass incarceration of Japanese Americans.

In Current Scholarship

Scholars interested in the influence of popular culture on Japanese-American relations have further examined the links between anti-Japanese racism and the US internment of Japanese Americans. Other scholars have examined Japanese war memories through cartoons known as manga,* as well as the American narrative of war in Disney movies. Some military historians, however, have criticized what they perceive as an overemphasis on the influence of culture, especially on the conduct of war. John Lynn,* a military historian at the University of Illinois, has emerged as a leading critic of *War Without Mercy*. Resisting Dower's arguments that US troops were motivated by anti-Japanese racism, Lynn offers alternative arguments based on classical theories of military history regarding combat motivation. For Lynn, "concern for comrades, desire for respect [and] acceptance of responsibility" motivates soldiers; racial hatred and viciousness do not.[6]

NOTES

1   Leo Braudy "Flags of Our Fathers/Letters From Iwo Jima," *Film Quarterly* 60, no. 4 (2007): 18.

2   Nina Cornyetz, "Fetishized Blackness: Hip Hop and Racial Desire in Contemporary Japan," *Social Text* 41 (1994).

3   John W. Dower, *Ways of Forgetting, Ways of Remembering: Japan in the Modern World* (New York: New Press, 2012), 28.

4   Roger Daniels, "Incarcerating Japanese Americans," *Organization of American Historians* 16, no. 3 (2002): 19.

5   Allan Austin, "Superman Goes to War: Teaching Japanese American Exile and Incarceration with Film," *Journal of American Ethnic History* 30, no. 4 (2011).

6   John A. Lynn, *Battle: A History of Combat and Culture* (New York: Basic Books, 2004), 252.

MODULE 11
IMPACT AND INFLUENCE TODAY

KEY POINTS

- *War Without Mercy* is an innovative work on the relationship between popular culture and Japanese-American relations during World War II.*

- Dower's approach challenges military historians, whose understanding of Japanese-American relations during World War II tends to be based firmly on military doctrines, strategy, technology, and warfare logistics.

- Although military strategists do not deny that popular culture is important, they generally argue that, rather than shaping violent behavior, it is a means by which soldiers on the battlefield cope with the horrors of war.

Position

In *War Without Mercy*, John Dower argues that the propagation of racist stereotypes through popular culture had a significant influence on the heinous conduct of both the Japanese and American militaries during World War II. According to Dower, this racial perception of the enemy contributed to misguided military intelligence, strategy, and the US decision to drop the atomic bomb on Hiroshima* and Nagasaki*—the first use of nuclear weapons in war.

To a great extent, Dower's arguments in *War Without Mercy* have become widely accepted by academic historians. Describing the Japanese and American conflict as one characterized by racist hatred and fear has become the most common interpretation of the Pacific War.* This is ironic, considering that at the time of publication Dower's cultural historical* method of inquiry was considered by

> **❝** All those who were beyond infancy at the time of Pearl Harbor know that racism was a powerful and malign element on both sides of the Japanese-American war, but this has receded from historical consciousness over the decades. John Dower … has brilliantly described and analyzed that racism in one of the handful of truly important books on the Pacific War … He has recreated the reciprocal stereotypes of the time and has shown their grim connection to the ruthlessness of that war. This is a cautionary tale for all peoples, now and in the future. **❞**
>
> Gaddis Smith,* "Review of *War Without Mercy*"

many scholars to be less than academic. However, Dower withstood these critiques and delivered the first critically acclaimed study of popular culture on Japanese-American relations during the war. Following in Dower's path, subsequent scholars of Japanese and American history have made use of evidence from popular culture and the guiding methodology of *War Without Mercy*.

Interaction

Military historians have traditionally opposed culture-focused analyses such as the one Dower presented. Rather, they foreground the study of military doctrines, strategy, technology, and warfare logistics. Studies of World War II following the cultural history approach typically neglect such in-depth examination of the battlefield, concerning themselves with the cultural products from the home front. John Lynn,* a leading military historian at the University of Illinois, writes that Dower and his disciples *imply* rather than *prove* that popular racial portrayals of the Japanese influenced US strategy and combat ethics in the Pacific War.*[1] In

Battle: A History of Combat and Culture, Lynn analyzes official military reports, strategy, and tactics, arguing that racism was an insignificant influence on the US conduct of war against Japan.

Dower has accepted the legitimate arguments leveled by military historians. He has, however, responded repeatedly to these concerns in introductions to "Race, Language, and War in Two Cultures," a widely reprinted essay that summarizes and expands the main arguments of *War Without Mercy.* As Dower explained most recently in 2012, "while racial thinking made both national solidarity and killing easier on all sides in the war in Asia, it is not my argument that racism is the key factor to understanding the cause or conduct of this conflict."[2] Here Dower engages constructively with the challenges advanced by some military historians, refining his conception of the Pacific War while retaining his main argument and defending his basic methodology.

The Continuing Debate

John Lynn is the most vocal opponent of the main arguments of *War Without Mercy.* In *Battle: A History of Combat and Culture,*[3] Lynn resists the characterization of the Pacific War as "a racial war," effectively questioning whether racism influenced combat motivation or overall US military strategy. In refuting Dower's main thesis, Lynn does not deny the prevalence of racism on the American home front, or in the language of American soldiers. In fact, Lynn readily cites the racist newsreels, movies, and cartoons that Dower first unveiled. However, Lynn does take aim at the lack of any investigation of the technical aspects of US strategy and doctrine by Dower and his proponents.[4] Further, he turns to more classical theories in military history concerning combat motivation, such as the sense of fraternity among soldiers, and of patriotic duty, asserting that racial hatred toward the opponent is not a significant driving factor—and that, furthermore, Dower's analysis furnishes evidence but not proof.[5]

Lynn offers an alternative theory to Dower's causal structure of racism. The anti-Japanese racial rhetoric of American soldiers, Lynn writes, did not cause the appalling killing of Japanese soldiers, but instead can be seen as a coping mechanism for soldiers dealing with the viciousness of the Pacific War.[6] In this interpretation, the dehumanization of the Japanese Other* was a way for American soldiers to come to terms with the scale of violence the battlefield necessitated. In closing, Lynn argues that the racism experienced on the American home front vastly differed from the racism on the battlefield. For Lynn, racism was not an influence on combat ethics or military strategy.

Lynn's arguments represent a wider trend within the rejection of Dower by military historians. Many military historians have similarly confronted Dower's thesis, arguing that racial stereotyping played a trivial role in the interpretation of military intelligence and the development of strategy. As one reviewer of Lynn's work stated, military history views cultural analysis as "flying in the face of battlefield decisions."[7] Strategic decision-making and the contingencies inherent in war are the primary influences on war conduct for military historians.

NOTES

1   John A. Lynn, *Battle: A History of Combat and* Culture (New York: Basic Books, 2004).

2   John W. Dower, *Ways of Forgetting, Ways of Remembering: Japan in the Modern World* (New York: New Press, 2012), 28–9.

3   Lynn, *Battle.*

4   Lynn, *Battle*, 237.

5   Lynn, *Battle,* 252.

6   Lynn, *Battle,* 256.

7   Wayne E. Lee, "Mind and Matter—Cultural Analysis in American Military History: A Look at the State of the Field," *The Journal of American* History 93, no. 4 (2007): 1117.

MODULE 12
WHERE NEXT?

KEY POINTS

- *War Without Mercy* will likely continue to serve as a foundation for future scholarship on Japanese-American history and relations, and the study of racism more broadly.

- The Asia-Pacific historian Takashi Fujitani's* book *Race for Empire* (2011) both employs Dower's approach and critiques several of Dower's specific points.

- Dower's exploration of the anti-Japanese racism that pervaded World War II* and its ramifications in contemporary American life is one of the most original accounts of the war between the United States and Japan.

Potential

John Dower's *War Without Mercy* continues to be relevant and significant for historians engaged in cultural studies. As an early practitioner of cultural history,* Dower paired his study of established sources of government documents and reports with less official sources, including music, film, cartoons, and popular writing. As Dower later wrote, cultural history had not been widely applied to Japanese history before *War Without Mercy*.[1] Cultural history was an emerging field in historical scholarship at the time of publication. As an early model of this now-established field, *War Without Mercy* remains a prominent and influential example of the significant perspectives gained through the study of cultural sources.

The arguments made in *War Without Mercy* hold great potential for further scholarship. While focused on the racial perceptions of the American and Japanese enemy, Dower also argues that the racist

“Anyone living in a peaceful time or place may find it surprising and even preposterous that nations at war should detest each other to the point where they commit horrendous atrocities against each other in the name of lofty ideals. But has that not been the case in all the major wars of this century?”

Ben-Ami Shillony,* "Review of *War Without Mercy: Race and Power in the Pacific War*"

language of the Pacific War* was not unique to the conflict between the United States and Japan. Instead, these racist stereotypes of the Other* are shown to have a long history preceding and following World War II. Such perceptions do not disappear once hostilities cool, but rather become the words used to describe the new enemy. This argument is ripe for further scholarship, leaving multiple paths open to a historical analysis of the influence of race and racial perceptions on the many wars of the past and present, and also the projected conflicts of the future.

Future Directions

One of the most important contributions by modern adherents of Dower's approach has been Takashi Fujitani's book *Race for Empire* (2011). Employing a comparative lens similar to Dower's, Fujitani analyzes both the experiences of Japanese Americans fighting for the US and Korean soldiers fighting for the Japanese during World War II. In doing so, Fujitani seeks to understand the experiences of soldiers fighting for a nation that discriminates against them. While *War Without Mercy* significantly influenced *Race for Empire*, it is Fujitani's refutation of many of Dower's arguments that mark this text as the most groundbreaking contribution among Dower's disciples. In his introduction, Fujitani praises Dower's comparative analysis of Japanese and American racism. But he also argues that Dower neglected to analyze the tension between the racist actions of both nations and the disavowals of racial motivations made in official public statements by their governments. As Fujitani states, the existence of Japanese and Korean soldiers in the militaries of the US and Japan respectively required "the official denunciation of racist discrimination."[2]

While both Japan and the United States practiced racial discrimination, Fujitani argues, official statements claiming racism did not exist still had real-life consequences for all those involved in the conflict. Finally, he contends that a major weakness in Dower's research is that it reproduces the idea that Japan and "white America" are two immutable and incompatible cultural units.

Summary

John Dower's *War Without Mercy* argues that popularly held racial stereotypes during World War II, perpetuated by newspapers, music, and movies, dehumanized both the American and Japanese enemy. In the minds of American and Japanese soldiers, military strategists, and the general public, the enemy was perceived to be savage, barbaric, and essentially subhuman. This sense of the subhuman Other was informed by depictions of beasts, monkeys, insects, and demons in popular culture. The result of this, as Dower argues, was a dehumanization and obsessive racial hatred of the Other, which advocated exterminating the enemy on both sides. War atrocities occurred throughout the conflict, as both Japanese and American soldiers slaughtered an enemy they believed to be undeserving of life.

War Without Mercy can be seen as a product of the political and social climate of the 1980s. During that period, Dower wrote a series of articles in American and Japanese publications in which he compared the racial language in World War II to that present in the developing economic tensions between the two countries. Dower found that similar patterns of racial stereotypes were re-emerging in the media. This essential link helps to solidify the pertinence of his argument and marks *War Without Mercy* as a major contribution to the growing field of cultural history, a challenging work in Japanese-American World War II relations, and a key advancement in studies of racism more broadly.

NOTES

1   John W. Dower, *Ways of Forgetting, Ways of Remembering: Japan in the Modern World* (New York: New Press, 2012), 28.

2   Takashi Fujitani, *Race for Empire: Koreans as Japanese and Japanese as Americans During World War II* (Berkeley: University of California Press, 2011), 16–18.

GLOSSARIES

GLOSSARY OF TERMS

Axis powers: the coalition headed by Germany, Italy and Japan that opposed the Allied powers in World War II.

Cold War: hostility between the United States and the Soviet Union that began after the end of World War II (1945) and continued until the fall of the Berlin Wall (1989) and the collapse of Soviet communism.

Committee of Concerned Asian Scholars (CCAS): a society founded in 1969 by graduate students from Harvard University, University of Michigan, University of California Berkeley, Stanford University, and Columbia University, united in their opposition to the Vietnam War and dedicated to the development of alternative studies of Asian culture.

Communism: a political ideology that relies on the state ownership of the means of production, the collectivization of labor, and the abolition of social class. It was the ideology of the Soviet Union (1917 to 1991), and contrasted to free-market capitalism during the Cold War.

Cultural history: is a sub-field of history that uses popular culture to explain historical experiences.

Democracy: a form of government in which power is devolved to citizens equally, usually through the right to vote to elect government representatives or to inform public policy.

Gulf War: the Gulf War (August 1990–February 1991) was fought between Iraq and a coalition of 39 nations, including the United States. It was the result of Iraq's invasion of Kuwait.

Hiroshima: the site of the first targeting of an atomic weapon, dropped by *Enola Gay,* an American bomber plane, on August 6, 1945. It has been estimated that over 80,000 Japanese were killed, while nearly 70 percent of Hiroshima's buildings were leveled.

Holocaust: the mass killing of Jews and groups including homosexuals and the disabled by the Nazis during World War II.

Imperialism: the extension of a nation's influence by territorial acquisition or by the establishment of political and economic dominance over other nations.

Iraq War: beginning in March 2003, the United States and United Kingdom (along with smaller contingents of forces from other nations) led the attack that resulted in the overthrow of Iraqi leader Sadaam Hussein. The US then withdrew its troops gradually between 2007 and 2011.

Manichean: the technique of looking at two things that are opposed (such as good and evil, light and dark, or love and hate).

Manga: a popular genre of Japanese cartoons.

Nagasaki: the bombing of Nagasaki, which had an estimated death toll of 40,000, occurred on August 9, 1945, three days after the bombing of Hiroshima. It was the last major act of World War II as the Japanese surrendered shortly after.

Nationalism: aggressively patriotic sentiment, or a political movement founded on a desire for self-determination (government).

Nazism: the extreme right-wing ideology of the Nazi party which, led by the dictator Adolf Hitler, governed Germany during World War II.

Other/Self-Other: Self-Other is a longstanding concept in the social sciences, popularized by the literary theorist Edward Said in his seminal work *Orientalism* (1978). Within its theoretical model, individuals' and groups' notion of the Other is constructed in opposition to the Self, or what they are.

Pacific War: the battles that took place in the Asia-Pacific region during World War II between 1941 and 1945.

Pearl Harbor: a Hawaiian harbor where the Japanese launched a surprise attack against a US naval base and other military installations on December 7, 1941; this catalyzed America's official entry into the war.

Postmodernism: an interdisciplinary philosophical movement that developed from the late twentieth century onwards. It represents a departure from modernism, and is marked by a distrust of grand narratives and Western-centric ideologies.

Spanish Inquisition: an institution that sought to safeguard the orthodoxy of Catholicism in Spain from the fifteenth to the seventeenth centuries. It persecuted Jews, Muslims, Protestants, and other groups.

Vietnam War: an armed conflict between communist North Vietnam and South Vietnam, on whose side the United States fought between 1960 and 1975, with the cost of many thousands of lives. The US decision to enter the conflict was motivated in large part to contain the spread of communism in South-East Asia.

World War II: a global war that occurred between 1939 and 1945.

PEOPLE MENTIONED IN THE TEXT

Henry Adams (1838–1918) was an American historian and member of the Adams political dynasty. His most important piece of scholarship was *The History of the United States During the First Administration of Thomas Jefferson* (1909).

Allan Austin is a professor of history at Misericordia University. He is a cultural historian.

Leo Braudy (b. 1941) is the Bing Professor of English at the University of California. He is a cultural historian and is best known for his books *The Frenzy of Renown: Fame and its History* (1986) and *From Chivalry to Terrorism: War and the Changing Nature of Masculinity* (2003).

George W. Bush (b. 1946) was the president of the United States between 2001 and 2009.

Nina Cornyetz is associate professor at the New York University Gallatin School of Individualized Study. She is a scholar of Japanese popular culture.

Roger Daniels (b. 1927) is professor emeritus of history at the University of Cincinnati. He is a scholar of Asian-American immigration and history.

Takashi Fujitani (b. 1953) is professor and director of the David Chu Program in Asia-Pacific studies, St. George Campus at the University of Toronto. He has written several influential books on Asian history, including *Race for Empire: Koreans as Japanese and Japanese as Koreans in World War II* (2011).

Adolf Hitler (1889–1945) was the leader of the German Nazi party from 1921, and chancellor of Germany from 1933 until his death by suicide in 1945.

John Lynn (b. 1943) is professor of history at the University of Illinois at Urbana-Champaign. He is the author of several important works on military history.

Iri Maruki (1901–95) and **Toshi Maruki (1912–2000)** were married Japanese artists who created large-scale joint paintings of the aftermath of the bombing of Hiroshima, Iri Maruki's home city.

Edgar Allan Poe (1809–49) was an American author and poet. He is famous for his tales and poems of horror and mystery, including *The Raven* (1845).

Theodore Roosevelt (1858–1919) was president of the United States from 1901 to 1909.

Edward Said (1935–2003) was a Palestinian American literary scholar and public intellectual. He published several seminal works, the most prominent of which is *Orientalism* (1978).

Yoshida Shigeru (1878–1967) was the prime minister of Japan from 1946 to 1947 and 1948 to 1954.

Ben-Ami Shillony (b. 1937) is professor emeritus at the Hebrew University of Jerusalem. He is a renowned scholar of Japanese history.

Gaddis Smith (b. 1932) is the Larned Professor Emeritus of History at Yale University. He has written several important works on American history, including *The Aims of American Foreign Policy* (1969).

Ronald Takaki (1939–2009) was a professor of history at the University of California at Berkeley and a scholar of racism.

George Washington (1732–99) was the commander-in-chief of the colonial forces during the American War of Independence and became the first president of the United States. He is widely regarded as one of America's founding fathers.

WORKS CITED

WORKS CITED

Allan, Austin. "Superman Goes to War: Teaching Japanese American Exile and Incarceration with Film." *Journal of American Ethnic History* 30, no. 4 (2011).

Braudy, Leo. "Flags of Our Fathers/Letters From Iwo Jima." *Film Quarterly* 60, no.4 (2007).

Cornyetz, Nina. "Fetishized Blackness: Hip Hop and Racial Desire in Contemporary Japan." *Social Text* 41 (1994).

Daniels, Roger. "Incarcerating Japanese Americans." *Organization of American Historians* 16, no. 3 (2002).

Dower, John W. "Art, Children and the Bomb." *Bulletin of Concerned Asian Scholars* 16, no. 2 (1984).

____. "Book Discussion: *Embracing Defeat*," C-Span, February 9, 2000. Accessed June 9, 2015, http://www.c-span.org/video/?155311–1/book-discussion-embracing-defeat.

____. *The Elements of Japanese Design: A Handbook of Family Crests, Heraldry, and Symbolism*. New York: Weatherhill, 1971.

____. *Embracing Defeat: Japan in the Wake of World War II*. New York: W. W. Norton & Co., 1999.

____. *Empire and Aftermath: Yoshida Shigeru and the Japanese Experience.* Cambridge: Harvard University Press, 1979.

____. "Japan and the US Samurai Spirit." *Bulletin of the Atomic Scientists* 47, no. 5 (1991).

____. "Japanese Artists and the Atomic Bomb." In *Japan in War and Peace: Selected Essays*, edited by John W. Dower. New York: New Press, 1993.

____. "Race, Language, and War in Two Cultures." In *Japan in War and Peace: Selected Essays*, edited by John W. Dower. New York: New Press, 1993.

____. "Racial Slurs Hurt Relations between Japan and the West," *Ottawa Citizen*, October 11, 1986.

____. "Sizing Up (and Breaking Down) Japan." In *The Postwar Developments of Japanese Studies in the United States*, edited by Helen Hardacre. Leiden: E.J. Brill, 1998.

____. "Triumphal and Tragic Narratives of the War in Asia." *Journal of American History* 82, no. 3 (1995).

____. *War Without Mercy: Race and Power in the Pacific War.* New York: Pantheon Books, 1993.

____. *Ways of Forgetting, Ways of Remembering: Japan in the Modern World.* New York: New Press, 2012.

Dower, John W., ed. *A Century of Japanese Photography.* New York: Pantheon, 1980

Fujitani, Takashi. *Race for Empire: Koreans as Japanese and Japanese as Americans During World War II.* Berkeley: University of California Press, 2011.

Hall, John W. et al., eds. *The Cambridge History of Japan*, 6 vols. Cambridge: Cambridge University Press, 1988-99.

Lee, Wayne E. "Mind and Matter—Cultural Analysis in American Military History: A Look at the State of the Field." *The Journal of American* History 93, no. 4 (2007).

Lu, David. "Review: War Without Mercy." *The Journal of Asian Studies* 46, no. 4 (1987).

Lynn, John A. *Battle: A History of Combat and* Culture. New York: Basic Books, 2004.

Olendorf, Donna et al., eds. *Contemporary Authors*. Detroit: Gale Research, 1992.

Said, Edward. *Orientalism.* London: Routledge & Kegan Paul, 1978.

Shillony, Ben-Ami. "Review of War Without Mercy," *Journal of Japanese Studies* 14, no. 1 (1988): 200–5.

Smith, Gaddis. "Review of War Without Mercy," *Foreign Affairs* (Fall 1986).

Takaki, Ronald. *Double Victory: A Multicultural History of America in World War II* (Boston: Little Brown, 2000).

____ *Hiroshima: Why America Dropped the Atomic* Bomb. Boston: Back Bay Books, 1996.

THE MACAT LIBRARY
BY DISCIPLINE

The Macat Library By Discipline

AFRICANA STUDIES

Chinua Achebe's *An Image of Africa: Racism in Conrad's Heart of Darkness*
W. E. B. Du Bois's *The Souls of Black Folk*
Zora Neale Huston's *Characteristics of Negro Expression*
Martin Luther King Jr's *Why We Can't Wait*
Toni Morrison's *Playing in the Dark: Whiteness in the American Literary Imagination*

ANTHROPOLOGY

Arjun Appadurai's *Modernity at Large: Cultural Dimensions of Globalisation*
Philippe Ariès's *Centuries of Childhood*
Franz Boas's *Race, Language and Culture*
Kim Chan & Renée Mauborgne's *Blue Ocean Strategy*
Jared Diamond's *Guns, Germs & Steel: the Fate of Human Societies*
Jared Diamond's *Collapse: How Societies Choose to Fail or Survive*
E. E. Evans-Pritchard's *Witchcraft, Oracles and Magic Among the Azande*
James Ferguson's *The Anti-Politics Machine*
Clifford Geertz's *The Interpretation of Cultures*
David Graeber's *Debt: the First 5000 Years*
Karen Ho's *Liquidated: An Ethnography of Wall Street*
Geert Hofstede's *Culture's Consequences: Comparing Values, Behaviors, Institutes and Organizations across Nations*
Claude Lévi-Strauss's *Structural Anthropology*
Jay Macleod's *Ain't No Makin' It: Aspirations and Attainment in a Low-Income Neighborhood*
Saba Mahmood's *The Politics of Piety: The Islamic Revival and the Feminist Subjec*t
Marcel Mauss's *The Gift*

BUSINESS

Jean Lave & Etienne Wenger's *Situated Learning*
Theodore Levitt's *Marketing Myopia*
Burton G. Malkiel's *A Random Walk Down Wall Street*
Douglas McGregor's *The Human Side of Enterprise*
Michael Porter's *Competitive Strategy: Creating and Sustaining Superior Performance*
John Kotter's *Leading Change*
C. K. Prahalad & Gary Hamel's *The Core Competence of the Corporation*

CRIMINOLOGY

Michelle Alexander's *The New Jim Crow: Mass Incarceration in the Age of Colorblindness*
Michael R. Gottfredson & Travis Hirschi's *A General Theory of Crime*
Richard Herrnstein & Charles A. Murray's *The Bell Curve: Intelligence and Class Structure in American Life*
Elizabeth Loftus's *Eyewitness Testimony*
Jay Macleod's *Ain't No Makin' It: Aspirations and Attainment in a Low-Income Neighborhood*
Philip Zimbardo's *The Lucifer Effect*

ECONOMICS

Janet Abu-Lughod's *Before European Hegemony*
Ha-Joon Chang's *Kicking Away the Ladder*
David Brion Davis's *The Problem of Slavery in the Age of Revolution*
Milton Friedman's *The Role of Monetary Policy*
Milton Friedman's *Capitalism and Freedom*
David Graeber's *Debt: the First 5000 Years*
Friedrich Hayek's *The Road to Serfdom*
Karen Ho's *Liquidated: An Ethnography of Wall Street*

John Maynard Keynes's *The General Theory of Employment, Interest and Money*
Charles P. Kindleberger's *Manias, Panics and Crashes*
Robert Lucas's *Why Doesn't Capital Flow from Rich to Poor Countries?*
Burton G. Malkiel's *A Random Walk Down Wall Street*
Thomas Robert Malthus's *An Essay on the Principle of Population*
Karl Marx's *Capital*
Thomas Piketty's *Capital in the Twenty-First Century*
Amartya Sen's *Development as Freedom*
Adam Smith's *The Wealth of Nations*
Nassim Nicholas Taleb's *The Black Swan: The Impact of the Highly Improbable*
Amos Tversky's & Daniel Kahneman's *Judgment under Uncertainty: Heuristics and Biases*
Mahbub Ul Haq's *Reflections on Human Development*
Max Weber's *The Protestant Ethic and the Spirit of Capitalism*

FEMINISM AND GENDER STUDIES

Judith Butler's *Gender Trouble*
Simone De Beauvoir's *The Second Sex*
Michel Foucault's *History of Sexuality*
Betty Friedan's *The Feminine Mystique*
Saba Mahmood's *The Politics of Piety: The Islamic Revival and the Feminist Subject*
Joan Wallach Scott's *Gender and the Politics of History*
Mary Wollstonecraft's *A Vindication of the Rights of Woman*
Virginia Woolf's *A Room of One's Own*

GEOGRAPHY

The Brundtland Report's *Our Common Future*
Rachel Carson's *Silent Spring*
Charles Darwin's *On the Origin of Species*
James Ferguson's *The Anti-Politics Machine*
Jane Jacobs's *The Death and Life of Great American Cities*
James Lovelock's *Gaia: A New Look at Life on Earth*
Amartya Sen's *Development as Freedom*
Mathis Wackernagel & William Rees's *Our Ecological Footprint*

HISTORY

Janet Abu-Lughod's *Before European Hegemony*
Benedict Anderson's *Imagined Communities*
Bernard Bailyn's *The Ideological Origins of the American Revolution*
Hanna Batatu's *The Old Social Classes And The Revolutionary Movements Of Iraq*
Christopher Browning's *Ordinary Men: Reserve Police Batallion 101 and the Final Solution in Poland*
Edmund Burke's *Reflections on the Revolution in France*
William Cronon's *Nature's Metropolis: Chicago And The Great West*
Alfred W. Crosby's *The Columbian Exchange*
Hamid Dabashi's *Iran: A People Interrupted*
David Brion Davis's *The Problem of Slavery in the Age of Revolution*
Nathalie Zemon Davis's *The Return of Martin Guerre*
Jared Diamond's *Guns, Germs & Steel: the Fate of Human Societies*
Frank Dikotter's *Mao's Great Famine*
John W Dower's *War Without Mercy: Race And Power In The Pacific War*
W. E. B. Du Bois's *The Souls of Black Folk*
Richard J. Evans's *In Defence of History*
Lucien Febvre's *The Problem of Unbelief in the 16th Century*
Sheila Fitzpatrick's *Everyday Stalinism*

The Macat Library By Discipline

Eric Foner's *Reconstruction: America's Unfinished Revolution, 1863-1877*
Michel Foucault's *Discipline and Punish*
Michel Foucault's *History of Sexuality*
Francis Fukuyama's *The End of History and the Last Man*
John Lewis Gaddis's *We Now Know: Rethinking Cold War History*
Ernest Gellner's *Nations and Nationalism*
Eugene Genovese's *Roll, Jordan, Roll: The World the Slaves Made*
Carlo Ginzburg's *The Night Battles*
Daniel Goldhagen's *Hitler's Willing Executioners*
Jack Goldstone's *Revolution and Rebellion in the Early Modern World*
Antonio Gramsci's *The Prison Notebooks*
Alexander Hamilton, John Jay & James Madison's *The Federalist Papers*
Christopher Hill's *The World Turned Upside Down*
Carole Hillenbrand's *The Crusades: Islamic Perspectives*
Thomas Hobbes's *Leviathan*
Eric Hobsbawm's *The Age Of Revolution*
John A. Hobson's *Imperialism: A Study*
Albert Hourani's *History of the Arab Peoples*
Samuel P. Huntington's *The Clash of Civilizations and the Remaking of World Order*
C. L. R. James's *The Black Jacobins*
Tony Judt's *Postwar: A History of Europe Since 1945*
Ernst Kantorowicz's *The King's Two Bodies: A Study in Medieval Political Theology*
Paul Kennedy's *The Rise and Fall of the Great Powers*
Ian Kershaw's *The "Hitler Myth": Image and Reality in the Third Reich*
John Maynard Keynes's *The General Theory of Employment, Interest and Money*
Charles P. Kindleberger's *Manias, Panics and Crashes*
Martin Luther King Jr's *Why We Can't Wait*
Henry Kissinger's *World Order: Reflections on the Character of Nations and the Course of History*
Thomas Kuhn's *The Structure of Scientific Revolutions*
Georges Lefebvre's *The Coming of the French Revolution*
John Locke's *Two Treatises of Government*
Niccolò Machiavelli's *The Prince*
Thomas Robert Malthus's *An Essay on the Principle of Population*
Mahmood Mamdani's *Citizen and Subject: Contemporary Africa And The Legacy Of Late Colonialism*
Karl Marx's *Capital*
Stanley Milgram's *Obedience to Authority*
John Stuart Mill's *On Liberty*
Thomas Paine's *Common Sense*
Thomas Paine's *Rights of Man*
Geoffrey Parker's *Global Crisis: War, Climate Change and Catastrophe in the Seventeenth Century*
Jonathan Riley-Smith's *The First Crusade and the Idea of Crusading*
Jean-Jacques Rousseau's *The Social Contract*
Joan Wallach Scott's *Gender and the Politics of History*
Theda Skocpol's *States and Social Revolutions*
Adam Smith's *The Wealth of Nations*
Timothy Snyder's *Bloodlands: Europe Between Hitler and Stalin*
Sun Tzu's *The Art of War*
Keith Thomas's *Religion and the Decline of Magic*
Thucydides's *The History of the Peloponnesian War*
Frederick Jackson Turner's *The Significance of the Frontier in American History*
Odd Arne Westad's *The Global Cold War: Third World Interventions And The Making Of Our Times*

LITERATURE

Chinua Achebe's *An Image of Africa: Racism in Conrad's Heart of Darkness*
Roland Barthes's *Mythologies*
Homi K. Bhabha's *The Location of Culture*
Judith Butler's *Gender Trouble*
Simone De Beauvoir's *The Second Sex*
Ferdinand De Saussure's *Course in General Linguistics*
T. S. Eliot's *The Sacred Wood: Essays on Poetry and Criticism*
Zora Neale Huston's *Characteristics of Negro Expression*
Toni Morrison's *Playing in the Dark: Whiteness in the American Literary Imagination*
Edward Said's *Orientalism*
Gayatri Chakravorty Spivak's *Can the Subaltern Speak?*
Mary Wollstonecraft's *A Vindication of the Rights of Women*
Virginia Woolf's *A Room of One's Own*

PHILOSOPHY

Elizabeth Anscombe's *Modern Moral Philosophy*
Hannah Arendt's *The Human Condition*
Aristotle's *Metaphysics*
Aristotle's *Nicomachean Ethics*
Edmund Gettier's *Is Justified True Belief Knowledge?*
Georg Wilhelm Friedrich Hegel's *Phenomenology of Spirit*
David Hume's *Dialogues Concerning Natural Religion*
David Hume's *The Enquiry for Human Understanding*
Immanuel Kant's *Religion within the Boundaries of Mere Reason*
Immanuel Kant's *Critique of Pure Reason*
Søren Kierkegaard's *The Sickness Unto Death*
Søren Kierkegaard's *Fear and Trembling*
C. S. Lewis's *The Abolition of Man*
Alasdair MacIntyre's *After Virtue*
Marcus Aurelius's *Meditations*
Friedrich Nietzsche's *On the Genealogy of Morality*
Friedrich Nietzsche's *Beyond Good and Evil*
Plato's *Republic*
Plato's *Symposium*
Jean-Jacques Rousseau's *The Social Contract*
Gilbert Ryle's *The Concept of Mind*
Baruch Spinoza's *Ethics*
Sun Tzu's *The Art of War*
Ludwig Wittgenstein's *Philosophical Investigations*

POLITICS

Benedict Anderson's *Imagined Communities*
Aristotle's *Politics*
Bernard Bailyn's *The Ideological Origins of the American Revolution*
Edmund Burke's *Reflections on the Revolution in France*
John C. Calhoun's *A Disquisition on Government*
Ha-Joon Chang's *Kicking Away the Ladder*
Hamid Dabashi's *Iran: A People Interrupted*
Hamid Dabashi's *Theology of Discontent: The Ideological Foundation of the Islamic Revolution in Iran*
Robert Dahl's *Democracy and its Critics*
Robert Dahl's *Who Governs?*
David Brion Davis's *The Problem of Slavery in the Age of Revolution*

The Macat Library By Discipline

Alexis De Tocqueville's *Democracy in America*
James Ferguson's *The Anti-Politics Machine*
Frank Dikotter's *Mao's Great Famine*
Sheila Fitzpatrick's *Everyday Stalinism*
Eric Foner's *Reconstruction: America's Unfinished Revolution, 1863-1877*
Milton Friedman's *Capitalism and Freedom*
Francis Fukuyama's *The End of History and the Last Man*
John Lewis Gaddis's *We Now Know: Rethinking Cold War History*
Ernest Gellner's *Nations and Nationalism*
David Graeber's *Debt: the First 5000 Years*
Antonio Gramsci's *The Prison Notebooks*
Alexander Hamilton, John Jay & James Madison's *The Federalist Papers*
Friedrich Hayek's *The Road to Serfdom*
Christopher Hill's *The World Turned Upside Down*
Thomas Hobbes's *Leviathan*
John A. Hobson's *Imperialism: A Study*
Samuel P. Huntington's *The Clash of Civilizations and the Remaking of World Order*
Tony Judt's *Postwar: A History of Europe Since 1945*
David C. Kang's *China Rising: Peace, Power and Order in East Asia*
Paul Kennedy's *The Rise and Fall of Great Powers*
Robert Keohane's *After Hegemony*
Martin Luther King Jr.'s *Why We Can't Wait*
Henry Kissinger's *World Order: Reflections on the Character of Nations and the Course of History*
John Locke's *Two Treatises of Government*
Niccolò Machiavelli's *The Prince*
Thomas Robert Malthus's *An Essay on the Principle of Population*
Mahmood Mamdani's *Citizen and Subject: Contemporary Africa And The Legacy Of Late Colonialism*
Karl Marx's *Capital*
John Stuart Mill's *On Liberty*
John Stuart Mill's *Utilitarianism*
Hans Morgenthau's *Politics Among Nations*
Thomas Paine's *Common Sense*
Thomas Paine's *Rights of Man*
Thomas Piketty's *Capital in the Twenty-First Century*
Robert D. Putnam's *Bowling Alone*
John Rawls's *Theory of Justice*
Jean-Jacques Rousseau's *The Social Contract*
Theda Skocpol's *States and Social Revolutions*
Adam Smith's *The Wealth of Nations*
Sun Tzu's *The Art of War*
Henry David Thoreau's *Civil Disobedience*
Thucydides's *The History of the Peloponnesian War*
Kenneth Waltz's *Theory of International Politics*
Max Weber's *Politics as a Vocation*
Odd Arne Westad's *The Global Cold War: Third World Interventions And The Making Of Our Times*

POSTCOLONIAL STUDIES

Roland Barthes's *Mythologies*
Frantz Fanon's *Black Skin, White Masks*
Homi K. Bhabha's *The Location of Culture*
Gustavo Gutiérrez's *A Theology of Liberation*
Edward Said's *Orientalism*
Gayatri Chakravorty Spivak's *Can the Subaltern Speak?*

PSYCHOLOGY

Gordon Allport's *The Nature of Prejudice*
Alan Baddeley & Graham Hitch's *Aggression: A Social Learning Analysis*
Albert Bandura's *Aggression: A Social Learning Analysis*
Leon Festinger's *A Theory of Cognitive Dissonance*
Sigmund Freud's *The Interpretation of Dreams*
Betty Friedan's *The Feminine Mystique*
Michael R. Gottfredson & Travis Hirschi's *A General Theory of Crime*
Eric Hoffer's *The True Believer: Thoughts on the Nature of Mass Movements*
William James's *Principles of Psychology*
Elizabeth Loftus's *Eyewitness Testimony*
A. H. Maslow's *A Theory of Human Motivation*
Stanley Milgram's *Obedience to Authority*
Steven Pinker's *The Better Angels of Our Nature*
Oliver Sacks's *The Man Who Mistook His Wife For a Hat*
Richard Thaler & Cass Sunstein's *Nudge: Improving Decisions About Health, Wealth and Happiness*
Amos Tversky's *Judgment under Uncertainty: Heuristics and Biases*
Philip Zimbardo's *The Lucifer Effect*

SCIENCE

Rachel Carson's *Silent Spring*
William Cronon's *Nature's Metropolis: Chicago And The Great West*
Alfred W. Crosby's *The Columbian Exchange*
Charles Darwin's *On the Origin of Species*
Richard Dawkin's *The Selfish Gene*
Thomas Kuhn's *The Structure of Scientific Revolutions*
Geoffrey Parker's *Global Crisis: War, Climate Change and Catastrophe in the Seventeenth Century*
Mathis Wackernagel & William Rees's *Our Ecological Footprint*

SOCIOLOGY

Michelle Alexander's *The New Jim Crow: Mass Incarceration in the Age of Colorblindness*
Gordon Allport's *The Nature of Prejudice*
Albert Bandura's *Aggression: A Social Learning Analysis*
Hanna Batatu's *The Old Social Classes And The Revolutionary Movements Of Iraq*
Ha-Joon Chang's *Kicking Away the Ladder*
W. E. B. Du Bois's *The Souls of Black Folk*
Émile Durkheim's *On Suicide*
Frantz Fanon's *Black Skin, White Masks*
Frantz Fanon's *The Wretched of the Earth*
Eric Foner's *Reconstruction: America's Unfinished Revolution, 1863-1877*
Eugene Genovese's *Roll, Jordan, Roll: The World the Slaves Made*
Jack Goldstone's *Revolution and Rebellion in the Early Modern World*
Antonio Gramsci's *The Prison Notebooks*
Richard Herrnstein & Charles A Murray's *The Bell Curve: Intelligence and Class Structure in American Life*
Eric Hoffer's *The True Believer: Thoughts on the Nature of Mass Movements*
Jane Jacobs's *The Death and Life of Great American Cities*
Robert Lucas's *Why Doesn't Capital Flow from Rich to Poor Countries?*
Jay Macleod's *Ain't No Makin' It: Aspirations and Attainment in a Low Income Neighborhood*
Elaine May's *Homeward Bound: American Families in the Cold War Era*
Douglas McGregor's *The Human Side of Enterprise*
C. Wright Mills's *The Sociological Imagination*

The Macat Library By Discipline

Thomas Piketty's *Capital in the Twenty-First Century*
Robert D. Putman's *Bowling Alone*
David Riesman's *The Lonely Crowd: A Study of the Changing American Character*
Edward Said's *Orientalism*
Joan Wallach Scott's *Gender and the Politics of History*
Theda Skocpol's *States and Social Revolutions*
Max Weber's *The Protestant Ethic and the Spirit of Capitalism*

THEOLOGY

Augustine's *Confessions*
Benedict's *Rule of St Benedict*
Gustavo Gutiérrez's *A Theology of Liberation*
Carole Hillenbrand's *The Crusades: Islamic Perspectives*
David Hume's *Dialogues Concerning Natural Religion*
Immanuel Kant's *Religion within the Boundaries of Mere Reason*
Ernst Kantorowicz's *The King's Two Bodies: A Study in Medieval Political Theology*
Søren Kierkegaard's *The Sickness Unto Death*
C. S. Lewis's *The Abolition of Man*
Saba Mahmood's *The Politics of Piety: The Islamic Revival and the Feminist Subject*
Baruch Spinoza's *Ethics*
Keith Thomas's *Religion and the Decline of Magic*

COMING SOON

Chris Argyris's *The Individual and the Organisation*
Seyla Benhabib's *The Rights of Others*
Walter Benjamin's *The Work Of Art in the Age of Mechanical Reproduction*
John Berger's *Ways of Seeing*
Pierre Bourdieu's *Outline of a Theory of Practice*
Mary Douglas's *Purity and Danger*
Roland Dworkin's *Taking Rights Seriously*
James G. March's *Exploration and Exploitation in Organisational Learning*
Ikujiro Nonaka's *A Dynamic Theory of Organizational Knowledge Creation*
Griselda Pollock's *Vision and Difference*
Amartya Sen's *Inequality Re-Examined*
Susan Sontag's *On Photography*
Yasser Tabbaa's *The Transformation of Islamic Art*
Ludwig von Mises's *Theory of Money and Credit*

Macat Disciplines

Access the greatest ideas and thinkers across entire disciplines, including

Postcolonial Studies

Roland Barthes's *Mythologies*
Frantz Fanon's *Black Skin, White Masks*
Homi K. Bhabha's *The Location of Culture*
Gustavo Gutiérrez's *A Theology of Liberation*
Edward Said's *Orientalism*
Gayatri Chakravorty Spivak's *Can the Subaltern Speak?*

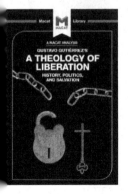
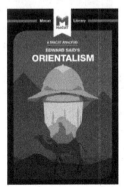

Macat analyses are available from all good bookshops and libraries.

Access hundreds of analyses through one, multimedia tool.
Join free for one month **library.macat.com**

Macat Disciplines

Access the greatest ideas and thinkers across entire disciplines, including

AFRICANA STUDIES

Chinua Achebe's *An Image of Africa: Racism in Conrad's Heart of Darkness*

W. E. B. Du Bois's *The Souls of Black Folk*

Zora Neale Hurston's *Characteristics of Negro Expression*

Martin Luther King Jr.'s *Why We Can't Wait*

Toni Morrison's *Playing in the Dark: Whiteness in the American Literary Imagination*

Macat analyses are available from all good bookshops and libraries.

Access hundreds of analyses through one, multimedia tool.
Join free for one month **library.macat.com**

Macat Disciplines

Access the greatest ideas and thinkers across entire disciplines, including

FEMINISM, GENDER AND QUEER STUDIES

Simone De Beauvoir's
The Second Sex

Michel Foucault's
History of Sexuality

Betty Friedan's
The Feminine Mystique

Saba Mahmood's
*The Politics of Piety:
The Islamic Revival and
the Feminist Subject*

Joan Wallach Scott's
*Gender and the
Politics of History*

Mary Wollstonecraft's
*A Vindication of the
Rights of Woman*

Virginia Woolf's
A Room of One's Own

Judith Butler's
Gender Trouble

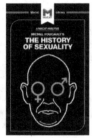

Macat analyses are available from all good bookshops and libraries.

Access hundreds of analyses through one, multimedia tool.
Join free for one month **library.macat.com**

Macat Disciplines

Access the greatest ideas and thinkers across entire disciplines, including

CRIMINOLOGY

Michelle Alexander's
*The New Jim Crow:
Mass Incarceration in the
Age of Colorblindness*

**Michael R. Gottfredson
& Travis Hirschi's**
A General Theory of Crime

Elizabeth Loftus's
Eyewitness Testimony

**Richard Herrnstein
& Charles A. Murray's**
*The Bell Curve: Intelligence and
Class Structure in American Life*

Jay Macleod's
*Ain't No Makin' It:
Aspirations and Attainment in a
Low-Income Neighborhood*

Philip Zimbardo's
The Lucifer Effect

Macat analyses are available from all good bookshops and libraries.

Access hundreds of analyses through one, multimedia tool.
Join free for one month **library.macat.com**

Macat Disciplines

Access the greatest ideas and thinkers across entire disciplines, including

INEQUALITY

Ha-Joon Chang's, *Kicking Away the Ladder*
David Graeber's, *Debt: The First 5000 Years*
Robert E. Lucas's, *Why Doesn't Capital Flow from Rich To Poor Countries?*
Thomas Piketty's, *Capital in the Twenty-First Century*
Amartya Sen's, *Inequality Re-Examined*
Mahbub Ul Haq's, *Reflections on Human Development*

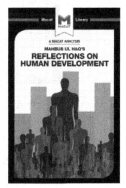

Macat analyses are available from all good bookshops and libraries.

Access hundreds of analyses through one, multimedia tool.

Join free for one month **library.macat.com**

Macat Disciplines

Access the greatest ideas and thinkers across entire disciplines, including

GLOBALIZATION

Arjun Appadurai's, *Modernity at Large: Cultural Dimensions of Globalisation*

James Ferguson's, *The Anti-Politics Machine*

Geert Hofstede's, *Culture's Consequences*

Amartya Sen's, *Development as Freedom*

Macat Disciplines

*Access the greatest ideas and thinkers
across entire disciplines, including*

MAN AND THE ENVIRONMENT

The Brundtland Report's, *Our Common Future*

Rachel Carson's, *Silent Spring*

James Lovelock's, *Gaia: A New Look at Life on Earth*

Mathis Wackernagel & William Rees's, *Our Ecological Footprint*

Macat analyses are available from all good bookshops and libraries.

Access hundreds of analyses through one, multimedia tool.
Join free for one month **library.macat.com**

Macat Disciplines

Access the greatest ideas and thinkers across entire disciplines, including

THE FUTURE OF DEMOCRACY

Robert A. Dahl's, *Democracy and Its Critics*
Robert A. Dahl's, *Who Governs?*
Alexis De Toqueville's, *Democracy in America*
Niccolò Machiavelli's, *The Prince*
John Stuart Mill's, *On Liberty*
Robert D. Putnam's, *Bowling Alone*
Jean-Jacques Rousseau's, *The Social Contract*
Henry David Thoreau's, *Civil Disobedience*

Macat analyses are available from all good bookshops and libraries.

Access hundreds of analyses through one, multimedia tool.
Join free for one month **library.macat.com**

Macat Disciplines

Access the greatest ideas and thinkers across entire disciplines, including

TOTALITARIANISM

Sheila Fitzpatrick's, *Everyday Stalinism*
Ian Kershaw's, *The "Hitler Myth"*
Timothy Snyder's, *Bloodlands*

Macat Pairs

Analyse historical and modern issues from opposite sides of an argument. Pairs include:

RACE AND IDENTITY

Zora Neale Hurston's
Characteristics of Negro Expression

Using material collected on anthropological expeditions to the South, Zora Neale Hurston explains how expression in African American culture in the early twentieth century departs from the art of white America. At the time, African American art was often criticized for copying white culture. For Hurston, this criticism misunderstood how art works. European tradition views art as something fixed. But Hurston describes a creative process that is alive, ever-changing, and largely improvisational. She maintains that African American art works through a process called 'mimicry'—where an imitated object or verbal pattern, for example, is reshaped and altered until it becomes something new, novel—and worthy of attention.

Frantz Fanon's
Black Skin, White Masks

Black Skin, White Masks offers a radical analysis of the psychological effects of colonization on the colonized.

Fanon witnessed the effects of colonization first hand both in his birthplace, Martinique, and again later in life when he worked as a psychiatrist in another French colony, Algeria. His text is uncompromising in form and argument. He dissects the dehumanizing effects of colonialism, arguing that it destroys the native sense of identity, forcing people to adapt to an alien set of values—including a core belief that they are inferior. This results in deep psychological trauma.

Fanon's work played a pivotal role in the civil rights movements of the 1960s.

Macat analyses are available from all good bookshops and libraries.

Access hundreds of analyses through one, multimedia tool.
Join free for one month **library.macat.com**

Macat Pairs

*Analyse historical and modern issues
from opposite sides of an argument.
Pairs include:*

INTERNATIONAL RELATIONS IN THE 21ST CENTURY

Samuel P. Huntington's
The Clash of Civilisations

In his highly influential 1996 book, Huntington offers a vision of a post-Cold War world in which conflict takes place not between competing ideologies but between cultures. The worst clash, he argues, will be between the Islamic world and the West: the West's arrogance and belief that its culture is a "gift" to the world will come into conflict with Islam's obstinacy and concern that its culture is under attack from a morally decadent "other."

Clash inspired much debate between different political schools of thought. But its greatest impact came in helping define American foreign policy in the wake of the 2001 terrorist attacks in New York and Washington.

Francis Fukuyama's
The End of History and the Last Man

Published in 1992, *The End of History and the Last Man* argues that capitalist democracy is the final destination for all societies. Fukuyama believed democracy triumphed during the Cold War because it lacks the "fundamental contradictions" inherent in communism and satisfies our yearning for freedom and equality. Democracy therefore marks the endpoint in the evolution of ideology, and so the "end of history." There will still be "events," but no fundamental change in ideology.

Printed in the United States
by Baker & Taylor Publisher Services